Launch
into the
Deep

A Scriptural Retreat

Anthony Bannon, LC

CIRCLE
PRESS

Circle Press
PO Box 5425
Hamdcen, CT 06518
www.circlepress.org

Printed in the United States of America

ISBN: 1-933271-09-4

CONTENTS

UNDERSTANDING OUR RETREAT

Starting Off Right

POTEMKIN'S VILLAGES

In 1787, several years after he annexed the southern lands as far as Crimea to the Russian Empire, Prince Gregory Potemkin wanted personally to show Catherine the Great the fruits of his campaigns, and no doubt enhance further his own high standing with her. So he put on a "royal show."

On his invitation, when it was still winter, Catherine traveled by sled from Moscow to Kiev, and once the Dnieper thawed she started on a long and fascinating journey down the river all the way to the Black Sea and Stevastopol.

There were seven floating palaces, eighty attendant vessels, and countless small supply boats shuttling supplies and people between them. As they passed through the countryside she could see the outlines of villages on the horizon, and in the middle distance the façades of well-painted and cared for houses. People worked the fields. Every day groups of riders dressed in their local costumes came to the river-bank to greet her and ride alongside. Everywhere she looked she saw evidence of industrious, prosperous, and happy communities. She was ecstatic and proud.

There was only one problem. It was all a show, literally. The towns she saw silhouetted in the distance were fake, uninhabited. The bright houses she saw in the middle distance were like Hollywood sets facing her, at times self-standing and at others hiding ruined hovels, with cardboard roofs and a coat of paint. The workers in the fields, the passing horsemen, the dancers in the villages in the evenings were the same people, shipped ahead regularly to set up their daily show for the empress in new costumes, in a new place.

Potemkin orchestrated all the entertaining aboard the floating palaces, and the empress never set foot on the shore to enter the towns she passed. The charade lasted the whole summer, and the empress was delighted and dazzled when she returned to St Petersburg, never having seen the truth. For example, the mighty fortress of Kherson that so impressed her was built entirely of sand, incapable of withstanding its first thunderstorm, never mind the attack of an enemy!

AND US...

Frequently, our dealings with God are reminiscent of Potemkin's show. We set out to make a good impression, but we don't want him too close. We stand on the bank to wave as he sails by on a Sunday morning, without disturbing either himself or us too much in the process.

THE GOSPEL

It's kind of like a passage in the Gospel. *"Two men went up to the temple to pray..."* and Jesus goes on to tell the parable of the Pharisee and the Publican. The Pharisee spent his prayer showing off to God, telling him what he wanted him to know, showing him the painted façade of his "justice." The Publican, however, invited God in. "Lord, look at my life, it's a mess. I need your forgiveness and mercy." And Jesus tells us that this is what prayer (and therefore a retreat) is really about. Inviting God in. Taking away the mask.

SO, OUR RETREAT

We want to make sure that Christ does not pass us by. We want him to stop. We want him to come in. We say, "Lord, this is what I am really like, this is the inside of my house. Tell me what you want changed, help me to change it."

A retreat is our attempt to break through the barriers we set up to keep God "satisfied" and ourselves undisturbed.

A retreat is not our opportunity to parade before God while at the same time keeping him at bay, convincing ourselves everything is fine, and perhaps thinking we have convinced him too.

A retreat is to throw open to him the doors of our hearts, our minds, our whole life and all its goings-on, and to invite in the Christ who is passing by. We don't want him to be a passing stranger—famous, powerful, well-known, but a stranger nonetheless.

We want him to come in, to check every corner of our house and to tell us what he likes and doesn't like, what is fine as it is and what needs changing, what is unsafe and needs fixing.

A retreat is to give him the run of our house.

HOW WE WILL DO OUR RETREAT

This retreat is made up of a series of chapters called meditations grouped in sections of varying lengths. Each meditation is a guided reflection on a Scripture passage. Each one follows the same pattern so as to help you as you do your retreat to learn one way of doing personal, meditative prayer. The emphasis is on stimulating your own conversation with Christ.

In each meditation, we prepare our soul through acts of faith, hope, and love. We then take and read the Scripture passage with the respect it deserves because it is the word of God.

We reflect on it, letting its message surface and opening our hearts to what God is telling us.

We compare our life and thinking with what we see in the Scripture, and we ask God to help us with his grace to change us into what he wants us to be.

HOW TO USE THIS BOOK

This book is not written to be read straight through. The ideal way to do it, at least once, is to take one meditation at a time, in the order in which they are presented in the book—no more than one a day, unless you really have time—reading over it slowly, thinking and conversing with God, letting him work in your soul.

A Short Primer on Prayer

A BRIEF EXPLANATION ABOUT PRAYER AND
THE METHOD WE WILL FOLLOW IN OUR RETREAT

PRAYER

To pray is to converse with God, who loves us. As in any conversation it involves at least two people, and it involves more than just their minds. When you have a really satisfying conversation you get to know the other person better, you connect not only with your mind but on every level, and more often than not you learn something new, or at least you become more aware of and understand better what you already know. And you usually can't wait for the next chance to chat again. In prayer, you converse with God, so you open to him not only your mind and understanding but also your heart. You converse with God, so you are ready to learn and to be changed by the experience. If you listen to him you learn his approach to life, the things that matter to him, how he would like you to act.

When you converse you give the other person his proper place. You don't deal the same way with your parents as you do with your coach or teammate. So as you pray, you need to be aware of who you are and who the person you are talking to is.

If you have a need and know someone who can help you with it, you ask him for his help, knowing that whether he gives it or not will depend on what he thinks about what you want to do. If he knows about finances and you are asking him for money to invest in a certain project, you know he won't give it to you if he knows the idea is worthless.

If you are with a person you admire or are indebted to, you will find ways to express your admiration and to thank him for what he gave you, and you will promise to pay him back.

All of this happens in prayer, but I think the single most important thing about prayer that we often forget is that we pray in order to be changed and enriched. We pray so as to learn and to get strength. We pray to learn the ways of Christ and to "deprogram" ourselves from the ways of the world; i.e., the ways of our human nature operating without the light of faith and more often than not under the effects of sin.

PRAYER AND PRAYERS

Prayers, (those prayers we learn by heart like the *Our Father,* the *Hail Mary,* the *Act of Contrition,* etc…) are very helpful in order to learn to pray, although saying prayers and praying are not necessarily the same thing. They are when we mean what we say, or when we try to mean what we say.

For example, we often pray "forgive us our trespasses as we forgive those who trespass against us." If we think about it, these are risky words. So, if we think about them as we say them, it reminds us how much we need to change our behavior, how different God's will is from our natural inclinations, and how much help we need in order to behave as he wants us to. When we want to change and we ask him to help us be what he wants us to be, we are praying.

So, prayers are very helpful. When we don't know what to pray for, when we are not sure what would please God, when we think God is asking too much of us…, our prayers teach us, they put the right words in our mouth, and they become the jump start of change in our heart.

Outline for Each Meditation

WHAT FOLLOWS IS THE DESCRIPTION OF THE STEPS WE WILL TAKE
IN EACH MEDITATION. IT IS AN OUTLINE THAT YOU CAN EASILY
LEARN AND APPLY IN YOUR OWN PERSONAL PRAYER.

I. RENEW THE PRESENCE OF GOD

We don't make him present (he already is), but we become aware
of his presence by making acts of faith, hope and charity. The retreat
this book is based upon was preached in the presence of the Blessed
Eucharist, and so I chose to leave these spontaneous prayers to Christ
really present in the Eucharist as they were, hoping they help you.

II. READ THE SCRIPTURE PASSAGE

It is God's word, and it has its own power. Read it slowly and
open your mind and heart to its message.

III. EXPLORE THE MEANING
AND MESSAGES OF THE PASSAGE

To do this, you engage actively your mind, memory, and
imagination. Under this heading, the meditations that follow provide
a series of numbered points to bring out some of the meaning and
applications suggested in the Scripture passage. However, there is
much more in each passage than what you will read here, so I invite
you to continue the exploration yourself and also to enrich your
understanding by reading other commentaries as well.

IV. DRAW SOME CONCLUSIONS

Connect the Scripture message with your life. Examine particularly how the message of the passage applies to you in your present situation.

V. COLLOQUIES

These are spontaneous conversations with Jesus, the Father, and the Holy Spirit. The thoughts given at this stage of the meditation are merely suggestions; you probably will have lots more you want to say yourself.

AND NOW...

Let us enter right away into prayer, starting with a meditation that will lead us into our retreat and set the premises for it.

Surprised by God

ZACCHAEUS IN LUKE 19:1-10

ENTERING INTO THE PRESENCE OF GOD

Lord Jesus, I thank you for the great gift you gave me in baptism, the gift of being able to believe. My senses see no more than the appearance of bread, and yet I know, I know for sure, without any chance of making a mistake, that you are here present—body, blood, soul and divinity—before me in the Eucharist. I believe your Holy Spirit inhabits my soul through grace.

I come before you as I start my retreat with a heart full of trust and hope. I know you will speak directly to my soul through the words of this retreat, and I know and trust that you will give me the light I am seeking in this retreat. I trust you because you love me and you know what I need even before I ask for it.

I often tell you I love you. But in this retreat I come to you to purify and renew my love. My love is so poor, so inconstant, so superficial. I want to spend this time with you, listen to you, let your word penetrate my heart as I look once more at your example, so you can transform me and teach me how to love truly, as you have loved me. I come to have my love renewed.

I thank you, Lord. If I have taken a weekend out to be with you, then I can say that you have also "taken this weekend" especially to be with me. I thank you for that. I thank you for all the circumstances that have led me here. I know every good thing comes from you.

You gave me Mary to be my mother. So in this retreat I'll take her hand once more, and I'll ask her to teach me what to do and how to listen. And I will listen to her as she says, "Do whatever he tells you."

SCRIPTURE PASSAGE

"He entered Jericho and was going through the town and suddenly a man whose name was Zacchaeus made his appearance; he was one of the senior tax collectors and a wealthy man. He kept trying to see which Jesus was, but he was too short and could not see him for the crowd; so he ran ahead and climbed a sycamore tree to catch a glimpse of Jesus who was to pass that way. When Jesus reached the spot he looked up and spoke to him, 'Zacchaeus, come down. Hurry, because I am to stay at your house today.' And he hurried down and welcomed him joyfully. They all complained when they saw what was happening. 'He has gone to stay at a sinner's house,' they said. But Zacchaeus stood his ground and said to the Lord, 'Look, sir, I am going to give half my property to the poor, and if I have cheated anybody I will pay him back four times the amount.' And Jesus said to him, 'Today salvation has come to this house, because this man too is a son of Abraham; for the Son of man has come to seek out and save what was lost.'"

EXPLORE THE MEANING
AND MESSAGES OF THE PASSAGE

Let us begin by looking for what was in Zacchaeus's mind, what his intentions were, and then we will shift perspectives and look at the scene with Jesus' eyes. The result will be an idea of what is actually happening to us on this retreat, beyond the appearances.

1. How did Zacchaeus know about Christ?

We get a possible answer by going to Luke 5:27-32.

"When he went out after this, he noticed a tax collector, Levi by name, sitting at the tax office, and said to him, 'Follow me. And leaving everything Levi got up and followed him. In his honor Levi held a great reception in his house, and with them at table was a large gathering of tax collectors and others. The Pharisees and their scribes complained to his disciples and said, 'Why do you eat and drink with tax collectors and sinners?' Jesus said to them in reply, 'It is not those that are well who need the doctor, but the sick. I have come to call not the upright but sinners to repentance.'"

Levi was a tax collector, so what happened to him may explain something about Zacchaeus. These two men were in the same despised profession of tax collectors. News of this extraordinary event of Levi and of Jesus' kindness would travel fast through their brotherhood.

2. Zacchaeus' purpose

What was on Zacchaeus' mind that day? Something very simple: to see who Jesus was. He heard Jesus was coming; he was making his way through all the towns. He was the new prophet, the one who welcomed sinners. He wasn't like the scribes or Pharisees. His heart was open to men like Levi and Zacchaeus. All he wanted to do was "to see which Jesus was." He was curious to see what kind of man Jesus was.

This is the sum total of Zacchaeus's plan when he suddenly makes his appearance.

3. Portrait of Zacchaeus

The Gospel tells us some things about him, and we can figure out others. Zacchaeus was one of the senior tax collectors and found it difficult to see Jesus. He couldn't see over the crowd because he was too short. He was a despised tax collector, so he had no friends to let him through. He was a rich man and short; probably plump and soft; no laborer, used to plenty of good food; well dressed, of course – rich people dressed well, at least up to our days. That's the external portrait.

But there is more to the man than this. He was not deterred by the unfriendly elbows or by his height that made it impossible to get through or see over the crowd.

His stubborn, hard-nosed side that made him such a successful tax collector surfaces, and what does he do? Something totally unexpected for a short, pudgy, soft, rich gentleman dressed in his Armani best. He goes and climbs a tree. He probably needed somebody to give him a boost up to reach the lower branches; maybe some kid made a quarter out of it. He wanted to see who this Jesus was, but there was a problem and the tree seemed like the only way. Nobody pushes Zacchaeus around; what he wants, he gets, and no apologies.

4. Zacchaeus has all he wants

Now as far as Zacchaeus is concerned, as he sits in that tree holding on for dear life and watching Jesus approach, he has all he wants. They tried to stop him and he won. He is doubly happy and satisfied. His plans are complete.

He can see the approaching crowd, the rising dust. He's the man in the middle, the disciples around him opening a path, the sick begging to be cured. Maybe some Pharisees are shouting questions at Jesus to see if he would answer them.

Ah, so that's Jesus, the man who got Levi, the one who pardons sinners. If you were to ask Zacchaeus, "Is there anything else you want?" he would happily answer, "No, I got what I wanted. I just wanted to see who he was."

5. Enter Jesus... A new development

When Jesus reaches the spot, he looks up and blows everyone's mind, especially Zacchaeus'. He says, "Zacchaeus, come down. Hurry, because I am to stay at your house today."

I've never met him before—how come he knows my name? The man whom Zacchaeus had never met before and had no idea even what he looked like, stops under his tree, looks up, and calls him by name.

So, Zacchaeus didn't know Jesus, but Jesus knew him. And then Jesus said, "Because today I'm going to stay at your house." And that seemed to be the whole purpose for the encounter.

It wasn't why Zacchaeus climbed the tree, but it was why Jesus stopped under it.

6. Jesus steps on a few toes

Now, who knows how many people along the way had invited Jesus to come to their house. It would be a blessing to have a prophet stay at your home.

But Jesus picks Zacchaeus, and everybody else begins to murmur and grumble. "There he goes with those sinners again." And the Gospel tells us they all complained.

7. Zacchaeus' discovery

Zacchaeus couldn't believe his luck. He hurries down, rushes to his home, gives the orders to his servants, and is at the door to *welcome*

Jesus joyfully when he arrives. His smug satisfaction as he sat in the tree has no comparison with his immense joy now because Jesus was coming into his house.

8. Yours too

You have come on retreat. I am sure it was not easy to get here. There were things you had to leave, arrangements you had to make, but you came. Right now you may be like Zacchaeus in the tree. Glad you came, but not knowing what comes next.

Listen to Jesus as he now stops in front of you, looks at you, and says, "I am going to stay with you today."

Zacchaeus might have asked himself later, "What drove me to look for Jesus? What drove me to make the effort and overcome the obstacles? It wasn't just me. It wasn't just that I wanted to see Jesus; it was that Jesus wanted to see me. That was the force that drove me."

So the real explanation for you being on this retreat is because Jesus has brought you. It wasn't just your doing. He wants to be with you and spend this time with you.

What seemed like a coincidence was actually Jesus' plan. Jesus has a hidden plan that picks up on ours and carries it much further than we expected or imagined.

This retreat is "Jesus seeking me" rather than "me seeking Jesus." And Jesus wants to give himself to me more generously than I could ever hope or wish for. Just like Zacchaeus. All he wanted to do was to see Jesus. He couldn't imagine Jesus spending time with him, knowing his name, yet that is what happened.

9. The real truth about a retreat

So a retreat is always a surprise. We get into it and suddenly the dimensions of what God wants, how far his grace can reach, and what he can do catches us completely by surprise as we go through our retreat. Because it is a matter of what God wants to do with us rather than what we came here to do for God.

And that's not all.

What happens when all these people complain and murmur? When the same thing happened at Levi's house the disciples didn't know what to say and Jesus had to answer for them. With Zacchaeus, things were different; he actually seems to be a few steps ahead of the apostles.

10. Zacchaeus, a changed man

Zacchaeus is still overwhelmed that Jesus would come into his house. No Pharisee would dream of eating with him, forgiving him, or defending him. Yet Jesus comes to his house. And what does he get in return but all this criticism.

Something happens between him and Jesus. The Gospel says here, "Zacchaeus stood his ground." Again, here is the strength of character that is not put off by difficulties or opposition.

Zacchaeus stood his ground. He wasn't going to be pushed around or let Jesus be pushed around. You can see what is going on inside his mind: "These people here are giving it to Jesus because I am a sinner and he's been kind to me. I am going to show him and them it was no mistake." He addresses Jesus out loud, so everyone else can hear. "I'm going to give half of my wealth to the poor." It could almost be a challenge. "So, I'm a sinner? Let's see you match this." But at the same time this says to Jesus, "You did not make a mistake coming into my house. Looking at you, I have changed. Seeing what you are willing to do for me has changed what I am willing to do for others." And so he adds, "If I have cheated anyone, come here, and I will pay you back four times as much."

Zacchaeus is standing up for Jesus. Zacchaeus is going to be as generous as Jesus was with him.

11. Zacchaeus discovers real love

Later on St. Paul would use one of the hymns of the early church to describe Jesus: he didn't hold onto his wealth, *he emptied himself, taking the form of a slave…, he was humbler yet, even to accepting death, death on a cross.* It's almost as if Zacchaeus is saying, "I want to be like you; just like you left everything, I am prepared to leave everything. I want to give generously to those around me."

What transformed him from a pitiless, remorseless tax-collector into this new man? Not Jesus' preaching—there was no preaching, just a meal, just his example. He *experienced* what Jesus was like, he *listened* to Jesus, he *saw* what Jesus did.

Under the influence of that example, Zacchaeus made options that if you'd asked him as he ran out the door that morning to see Jesus, he wasn't even considering. "Is it true you're going to give away half of what you own to the poor today?" He probably would have found such a bizarre idea quite hilarious.

It is not unusual in a retreat when we come face-to-face with Jesus, taking time to really look at him, that we make decisions that are otherwise inexplicable, but which make us so much more like Jesus than we are now.

SUMMARY

Zacchaeus went out simply wanting to see Jesus. Then he discovered that Jesus wanted to see him. So he welcomed Jesus into his house and discovered his love. That put his whole life into perspective, and Zacchaeus became a new man.

CONCLUSIONS

Here we have a pattern for our retreat. We have to realize it was not so much a question of us coming as Jesus inviting us.

Let Jesus, right here and now, tell you he wants to be with you. Come down from your comfort, welcome him in, and use the time he is with you to learn from him and be changed by him.

What we're trying to do is get to know Christ, get to know God, to get to know the gifts that God has given us. And that will make this retreat fruitful.

Because if we get to touch the love of God, if we open our soul and let him work in our soul, we will see how God has loved us. Then things we may have hesitated about will suddenly sound very logical to us, the only way to go. This is where we will find the strength to make those decisions we want to make and came on this retreat to make.

COLLOQUIES

So, pray... Take a few minutes on your own; be here in the presence of Christ in the chapel for a while to relive Zacchaeus' story and open your heart to Jesus.

God, you brought me here. I don't know how you are going to speak to me in this retreat, but I do know one thing: if I knew you better I would probably love you more. If I knew you better and loved you a little more, certain things would probably not have as much of a hold on me as they do now. I would not be the hesitant, doubting person I am now.

⊠ ⊠ ⊠

Initial Questionnaire

Although the following is in the form of a questionnaire, your purpose in answering it is not so much to "get the right answers" as to reflect in God's presence at the beginning of your retreat on what it means to have been called to spend this time with him. It should help you to approach your retreat from the point of view of faith and to adopt an attitude of openness and effort, which will help you make the most of the special graces God has in mind to grant you.

It may help to take pen and paper and jot down your reflections as you work through the points. Better still, start a journal for the days of this retreat, writing down your personal reflections and insights as you move through it.

1. Why did I decide to do this retreat? What fruit have I gotten from previous retreats?

2. If going on a retreat is like Zacchaeus climbing the tree (the wonderful part is not so much my intentions as God's) and a personal invitation from Christ, why do I think God wants me to do this retreat?

3. What have my dealings with Christ been like up to now? Have I been keeping him at a distance, putting on a show for him?

4. What are my dispositions now? Am I ready to open my doors for Christ to come in and check everything? Is there anything

I hope he doesn't see...or ask for? What am I most nervous about—as regards my life in general and as regards this retreat?

Take a moment to make an act of faith and trust in Christ. Write it in your own words. Place your retreat in his hands.

5. What is the big question I would like answered during this retreat? What is the most urgent thing to adjust/correct/change in my life? Or am I not figuring on changing anything?

6. Take a closer, more practical look at your dispositions:

   - Do I realize that, although the retreat is a grace from God, it will take effort on my part to bear the fruit it is meant to?
   - How willing am I to dedicate myself to the prayer, silence, and reflection that will make it fruitful?
   - Do I really believe that this retreat will be the beginning of something new in my life?
   - Are my feelings working in favor of the retreat, or do I have to overcome them?
   - Am I willing to go into depth in each meditation, and use it to the best?
   - Will I go beyond simply reading this book, and speak to God in depth and earnestly about the points he brings up for my reflection?

7. Make your resolutions as regards the retreat in a personal note to Christ.

PART I

We will start our retreat by reflecting God and us. We will seek to know who he is and who we are, what our relationship with him is; what we are made of, what we are made for, why we value freedom so much, and what is its true place. We will discover just how important love is.

We could try to do all this through abstract and philosophical reasoning, but that is a path fraught with difficulty, as any history of philosophy can attest. It is like searching in a dark room with a match, when all we need to do is open the shutters to let the sun shine in.

So, in our retreat we are going to listen to God explain his actions to us in his own words. We will take the images and stories the Holy Spirit uses in Scripture and let him speak to us through them.

❖ ❖ ❖

The Gift and Mystery of Life
THE AMAZING MOTHER AND HER SONS, 2 MACCABEES 7

RENEW THE PRESENCE OF GOD

Lord Jesus, I come before you on this day of retreat—a day I have set aside for you, and also a day you have set aside just for me. Thank you.

I believe that you are really present here in the Eucharist, body and blood, soul and divinity, with the same power and presence as when you walked the earth with your apostles, when you died on the cross to save us from our sins, and gave yourself, your body and your blood to us in the Last Supper. I believe, Lord, increase my faith. If I had faith like a mustard seed, nothing would be impossible to me. My faith may be even smaller, but it has allowed me to choose you above anything else this weekend. I believe you are here calling me by name; you wish to enter my home and to give yourself to me in this retreat.

I hope in you. I know that my life has only one meaning and one sense, and that is to use it well so that one day I will join you forever in heaven in the company of your saints. And all this life has to offer is nothing compared to the joy that you have prepared for us in heaven. I hope to reach that joy one day, and I know that each day of my life now is a step. Today, this time with you, is a step closer to when I will see you without the veil of the Sacrament, and be immensely happy.

I love you, and I wish to love you more. The more I know about you and the closer I come to you, the more I realize how much you love me and how poor my love is. I come here this morning in humility knowing that my love has not always been what it should be, that there are other loves pulling at my heart. I know that in this retreat you are going to open your soul to me and have me see you as I've never seen you before. Increase my love so I can love you truly.

I thank **you** Lord for the time you spend with me, here in the Eucharist. I thank you for the faith I received through my family and the many other means that you have placed in my life. I thank you also for your trials and for your crosses because they have helped to purify me and bring me closer to you.

Mary, I take your hand. Guide me, show me by your example what your Son means. Teach me how to pray, teach me how to listen, to *do all that he tells me.* I place all my efforts in this retreat in your hands for you to purify them and make me worthy of Jesus your Son.

REMINDER: WHAT ARE WE DOING ON THIS RETREAT?

Sometimes we think that our faith is a question of knowledge, and the more we know, and the sharper our theological arguments, so much the better Christians will we be. Faith is not these things, and we are not going to try to make it the result of our explorations. Instead, it is always our starting point.

We are going to take Jesus, the Holy Spirit, as he speaks to us through his Scriptures. We are going to take these Scriptures with faith and examine them in the light of our faith. We're going to try to penetrate the mind and heart of God, to bring his light to bear on our lives—lives very often caught up in the day-to-day things, in our own small problems, small from the outside but everything for us. In our retreat we put it all in the perspective of God, we invite God to shine his light into our lives. We place all our doubts, struggles, and problems, our tendency to see things only our own way, under God's lamp.

We want to discover what God thinks about us, what God thinks about our lives, and yes, what God thinks about our future, so as to adjust what we do to what God thinks.

SCRIPTURE PASSAGE

Our first "window" on God will be from the Old Testament: 2 Maccabees, chapter 7. What follows are some highlights from the passage, but you would do good to read it all on your own. It is very eloquent regarding what we are here for, what our life is, and what is going to help and guarantee that those decisions that we make, the small steps that we take in our lives, will be founded in God.

"It also happened that seven brothers were arrested with their mother. The king tried to force them to taste some pork, which the Law forbids, by torturing them with whips and scourges. One of them, acting as spokesman for the others, said, 'What are you trying to find out from us? We are prepared to die rather than break the laws of our ancestors.' The king, in a fury, ordered pans and cauldrons to be heated over a fire. As soon as these were red hot, he commanded that their spokesman should have his tongue cut out, his head scalped and his extremities cut off, while the other brothers and his mother looked on. When he had been rendered completely helpless, the king gave orders for him to be brought, still breathing, to the fire and fried alive in a pan. As the smoke from the pan drifted about, his mother and the rest encouraged one another to die nobly, with such words as these, 'The Lord God is watching and certainly feels sorry for us, as Moses declared in his song, which clearly states that "he will take pity on his servants." When the first had left the world in this way, they brought the second forward to be tortured…. After him, they tortured the third… the fourth… the fifth…the sixth…

"But the mother…watched the death of seven sons in the course of a

single day, and bravely endured it because of her hopes in the Lord. Indeed she encouraged each of them... 'I do not know how you appeared in my womb; it was not I who endowed you with breath and life, I had not the shaping of your every part. And hence, the Creator of the world, who made everyone and ordained the origin of all things, will in his mercy give you back breath and life, since for the sake of his laws you have no concern for yourselves.'

"As the youngest was still alive (the king, Antiochus) appealed to him not with mere words but with promises on oath to make him both rich and happy if he would abandon the traditions of his ancestors; he would make him his friend and entrust him with public office. The young man took no notice at all, and so the king then appealed to the mother, urging her to advise the youth to save his life. After a great deal of urging on his part she agreed to try persuasion on her son. Bending over him, she fooled the cruel tyrant with these words, uttered in their ancestral tongue, 'My son, have pity on me; I carried you nine months in my womb and suckled you three years, fed you and reared you to the age you are now, and provided for you. I implore you, my child, look at the earth and sky and everything in them, and consider how God made them out of what did not exist, and that human beings come into being in the same way. Do not fear this executioner, but prove yourself worthy of your brothers and accept death, so that I may receive you back with them in the day of mercy.' She had hardly finished, when the young man said, 'What are you all waiting for? .... I too, like my brothers, surrender my body and life for the laws of my ancestors'.... The king fell into a rage and treated this one more cruelly than the others, for he was himself smarting from the young man's scorn. And so the last brother met his end undefiled and with perfect trust in the Lord. The mother was the last to die, after her sons."

EXPLORE THE MEANING
AND MESSAGES OF THE PASSAGE

1. The event

This passage speaks of a time of upheaval and persecution, a time when the service we give God is not in the serenity and beauty of the liturgy, but in the great battle of life, when fidelity comes at the price of our life. It is the way the faith, for the most part, has been handed down to us. Here, eight people make the supreme decision in their lives, and what we are going to discover in this passage is that their decision was not blind, but rather full of light.

2. Approaching the message

For those who torment them, there is no explanation for the actions of these young men and their mother. But as we hear them all speak, especially the mother, we discover what light and what security, and with what confidence and trust and hope they do what to everybody else seems like utter stupidity—suffering torture and throwing away their young lives.

3. The promises, the temptation

Let's go right to the last act of the drama. Six brothers have died. All six chose rather to obey God than the king. Each in turn was horribly maimed, tortured, and killed, and now there are two people left—the youngest son and his mother.

By now the king is getting desperate; he needs at all costs some sort of victory. Threats didn't work, so he changes his approach and tries to woo the young boy over: "As the youngest was still alive, the king appealed to him, not with mere words but with promises and oaths" (public promises that he could not go back on—remember Herod and Herodias' daughter in Mk 6:23). And he promised that he would *make him rich* and he would *make him happy* on condition *that he would abandon the customs of his forefathers*. He also promised that "he would make him his Friend and entrust him with public office, give him power. And when "the young man took no notice at all, the king appealed to the mother and urged her to advise her boy to save his life." And he "urged her for a long time," and then she went through the motions of persuading her son.

4. The temptations and the strength of the temptations

Look at the king's promises—they are the same ones the Devil tempts us with when he doesn't want us to do what God wants. And the king makes his promises on oath to prove he will not go back on them:

"I will make you rich." Money. How tempting. And the boy knows the king can deliver, the king can simply take the money from someone else and give it to him if he wants to.

"I will make you happy. All the pleasures of my court are there for your asking—food, drink, company, everything you want. I'll make you happy."

"I will make you my Friend and I will give you power. *I will give you public office."* In other words, "you will be safe, everyone will respect and fear you, no one will dare go against you because you are a Friend of the King. Everyone will bow and scrape before you." The king is promising everything.

Remember in the temptations of Jesus when the devil says to him, "Look at all these kingdoms of this world and all the power, everything has been given into my hands and I will give it to you if you fall down and adore me?" This king is making essentially the same boast. "Everything you see around you, all the power, all the riches, all the pleasures that are mine, I can give them to you." And he is asking the boy to fall down and adore him, to "just do as I want, reject your God, and follow me. I will give you all of these things."

5. The boy's reaction

He doesn't go for it. Worst of all from the king's point of view, he doesn't even seem to struggle with the idea. "He took no notice at all." If at least he had teetered, hesitated, bargained to settle on a price. Just like Jesus would later pay no attention, would never doubt, hesitate, or reconsider when the devil tempted him.

6. The ultimate appeal

As his last desperate attempt, the king turns to the boy's mother. "He appealed to the mother urging her to advise the youth to save his life." He seems to be begging now, asking her to talk some sense into her son. However, not without a subtle threat that could be phrased, "Think, woman, what will happen to you without a son to take care of you." Life for a childless widow in those times was inevitably one of poverty, hardship, and begging.

The results were not immediate. "After he had urged her for a long time, she went through the motions of persuading her son." And what follows is a truly wonderful, wonderful passage, in which we discover where (from whom) the seven sons got their faith, courage, and strength from, and how well she understood the heart of God.

7. The truth, the way things really are

"My son, have pity on me." She is the mother who has lost six sons and he is the only one left to her. It seems she is going to ask him for something. She starts by reminding him of all he owes her, "I carried you in my womb for nine months, I nursed you for three years. I brought you up, I educated you and I supported you to your present age." "Look at all I've done and gone through for you." I wonder what the young boy was making of all this, because right now it looks like she has changed and is going to ask him to save both their lives. "I beg you my child," and here she comes with her petition... "I beg you my child, look at the heavens and the earth and see all that there is in them. Then you'll know that God did not make them out of existing things, and in the same way human race came into existence. Do not be afraid of this executioner, be worthy of your brothers and accept death so that in the time of mercy I may receive you again with them!"

Isn't this extraordinary when you put yourself in her place? The father does not appear in the story so she probably was a widow. With seven fine strong sons she must have been the envy of her neighbors, her future was assured, someone would be there to take care of her as old age approached. Now in a single day she lost them all except the youngest. Instead of seeking her security and holding onto him she said, "Look at all around you, the heavens and the earth, look at the king. God made them all, including him, out of nothing. Choose well who you obey and who you follow."

8. Creation, the great lesson about life

Earlier on in verse 22, we have the words the mother used to encourage her sons in their agony, and these too are amazing and unexpected. "I do not know how you came into existence in my womb [yet she was their mother!], it was not I who gave you the breath of life, nor was it I who set in order the elements of which each of you is composed. Therefore since it is the creator of the universe who shapes each man's beginnings, as he brings about the origin of everything, he in his mercy will give you back both breath and life because you now disregard yourselves for the sake of his law."

Here is a woman speaking from experience. Instead of being possessive of her sons, she realized each one of them was a gift. She hadn't, couldn't have decided if they were going to be boys or girls, the color of their eyes, their intelligence or physical ability. Perhaps also she had the experience of a child that died young, or was stillborn. As she held it in her arms, wishing with all her heart she could make it breathe and live, she learned from bitter experience that she was not the one who ultimately gave life.

So where did this life that she nurtured in her womb come from?

She said, "It comes from God. God is the one who gave you life, God is the one who decided what you were going to look like. God is the one who chose each one of you. I didn't, even though I am your mother. I am not the source of your life; God is the source." And see now, how that truth helped her when she faced the greatest tragedy of her life.

For each one of us, the most dramatic decisions are not those taken by famous people in history, but the ones we ourselves have to make and which define our lives. Look at the dramatic decision this woman took seven times in one day. Seven times over she encouraged each of her sons to be faithful to without counting the cost to herself. She told each one of them, "You did not receive the gift of life from me, for I can't give you life, only God can. But if you are faithful to God, he is the one who is going to give you back your life. Only God the Creator and no one else can give you life."

9. The great discovery...

Here is this woman's truly remarkable intuition: "He in his mercy will give you back both breath and life because you now disregard yourselves for the sake of his law."

She says, "God is the source of life; he gave you the gift of life, and right now you are faced with a choice between the giver and the gift. Will you obey God and let go of the gift, or will you hold onto the gift and reject God, the giver?"

Then she makes this fabulous, intuitive leap into the very heart and mind of God and she says, in essence, "If God was so generous as to give you life and freedom in the first place, without you asking for them, purely because he wanted to give them to you, do you think he is going to turn his back on you if you sacrifice them for him? If you say to him with your actions, 'You are more important to me than your gifts,' is he just going to shrug his shoulders and turn away indifferently? No, he is going to be so moved that he will give you back the gift of "breath and life"—but a better, eternal life where we will all meet again."

So she says, "*Do not be afraid of this executioner, he is only a creature of God too, he cannot give you true life*, there is nothing he can take away that God cannot give back."

CONCLUSIONS

1. This woman put more trust in God who gave us life than in the promises of the king. So often in our struggles we're looking for life and fulfillment, but somewhere else outside of God, not trusting him, seeking to keep the gift rather than the giver.

2. When the world like this king promises us happiness, pleasure, power and riches, we have to ask, can the world deliver? Where it is the source of life? Where is our source of wealth? Where is our source of happiness? How lasting is it all? God is the creator. God is the one who gave us everything that we are. God is the only one worthy of our faith and absolute trust. He is the only one who can deliver and he is the only one who really wants to deliver on his promises.

3. The only good that will never fail us and the only promises that we can base our life on, are God's because he is the creator. He is the Lord. He is the one who gives life.

4. If we're truly convinced that we come from God, that he made us out of the earth, that he gave us his own breath, then we will be able to do what we're supposed to do, and not merely what is expedient. "Be strong and do not be afraid. This king who's

torturing you did not give himself life, he did not get it from his mother, he too got it from God; and at the end of his life he is going to have to stand before God, and tell God what he did with that life."

COLLOQUIES

Christ came to give us the eternal life that his Father created us to enjoy. Take some personal moments just speaking with Christ here in the Eucharist, reflecting on this wonderful passage, the attitude of the sons and the attitude of the mother. Let God's light find its way into your mind, accept it.

In comparison with Christ, nothing in this life is worth anything. In comparison with him, it is easy to give up life itself like these seven men and their mother.

Take some time with our Lord, open your soul and heart to this wonderful truth about the God who created us out of love, saved us out of love, is the source of life, and on whom we can always depend upon to come through on the promises he makes us.

Made of Matter and Spirit

GENESIS 2:7; 3:1-6

In our previous meditation we discovered the great truth behind our lives: God created us. This is a guiding truth, it is capable of steering us toward the right decisions, like the seven sons who gave their lives and knew God would not abandon them.

Now we are going to listen to God's own description of how he created us. This is important, for it will tell us much about ourselves.

ENTERING INTO THE PRESENCE OF GOD

Lord, I believe in you. You are the Creator, the source of all life. You made everything out of nothing. My life is a gift from you. Man would be powerless to transmit life if your power weren't behind his actions. Everything else is passing, you alone are forever.

How could I put my trust in anyone else? Why should I fear anyone else if you are what matters and you are faithful? If I am faithful to you, even at the cost of my life you will not abandon me, but will give me back life eternal.

Lord, I love you. You loved me first by giving me life. You thought of me and wanted me even before I existed. I owe you everything. I thank **you**, and want always to thank you.

Mary, "you proclaimed the greatness of the Lord, and rejoiced in him for he looked upon his lowly handmaid." Teach me to be humble, to contemplate his gifts and to praise him for them.

SCRIPTURE PASSAGE

"...there was as yet no wild bush on the earth nor had any wild plant yet sprung up, for Yahweh God had not sent rain on the earth, nor was there any man to till the soil. Instead, water flowed out of the ground and watered all the surface of the soil. Yahweh God shaped man from the soil of the ground and blew the breath of life into his nostrils, and man became a living being. *Yahweh God planted a garden in Eden, which is in the east, and there he put the man he had fashioned"* (Gen 2:5-7).

EXPLORE THE MEANING
AND MESSAGES OF THE PASSAGE

God gives us two different explanations of creation in the book of Genesis. This is one of them; our next meditation will focus on the other. When the Holy Spirit wants to describe how we were created, where we come from, and what we are made of, these are the words he chooses. Let us examine them carefully, respectfully. God has compressed into them a marvelous mystery.

1. A deeply personal, individual act

We have here a vivid picture of God, as it were, stooping down to scoop up some clay, molding and shaping it into a form of his liking. Then the gesture of bringing it close to his face, looking at it and deliberately breathing his own life-giving breath into it... and that rigid statue becomes alive.

There is nothing accidental about it. Nothing forced. It is God's free and deliberate action. It is personal.

This is where we need our faith to get beyond the limitations of our experience and imagination (which we sometimes call our reasoning). We cannot imagine being able to keep track of and having a personal interest in thousands of people, never mind millions and billions, and so we presume we are at the best just numbers for God. We imagine some sort of mass production on his part. But our faith teaches us that each soul is created individually by God at the moment life begins.

So the picture of the creation of the first man by God is also the picture of our creation. You and I are a fruit of this same creating love that breathed a soul into us at the very beginning of each one's existence, giving us life. Such is God's creating love.

Despite the most famous painting of *The Creation of Man* in the Sistine Chapel, God's explanation is different. It's not an impersonal reaching out to barely touch fingertip to fingertip. This image misses all the personal action of God, his involvement in forming that body, and the almost kiss of breathing into him a share in his own life. It is a face-to-face encounter and creation, rather than fingertip-to-fingertip.

2. Made from the dust of the earth

God is also letting us know what he made us of. He formed us from the dust of the earth. We are part of his material creation; we are matter, dust, clay. Part of us is truly from the earth. We should have no illusions about that. Dust from dust, and into dust we will return. Our concept of what this "dust" is may change as science investigates our material makeup and makes its discoveries, but the fact remains that there is a material part of us that shares the characteristics and laws of the rest of creation, and can be increasingly understood by applying the methods of science.

We are as subject to the law of gravity as a stone. We need nourishment like the plants and animals in order to stay alive and to grow. We tire, we need rest, and we need air. We have flesh and blood like the animals and share their instinct for survival....

If we ever forget that we are taken from material creation, we will never understand ourselves completely.

That's one thing God tells us in this passage.

3. The breath of God

But equally clear here is the fact that we may be matter, but we are much more as well. Matter alone, our material composition, does not explain what or who we are. It does not explain life. We have in us the breath of God, which makes us living beings. We are not only matter, we are spirit too. Not only does God tell us this, but it is also our experience.

We desire goodness, we desire beauty, we desire freedom, we want to rise above all that is petty and ugly. We want to be masters and not slaves. We want to love and be loved. Evil abhors us. We can think in terms of right and wrong. We do not want to die. Good actions attract and inspire us.

This is the breath of God at work in us.

4. The uncomfortable coexistence

Our material and spiritual natures are radically different from each other. We could say they are two different worlds. Our experience tells us that there are two poles in our lives, two opposite attractions, two laws, each one laying claim to us.

Sometimes we tend to attribute all the division we feel within us solely to sin. But while it is true that sin is at work in us and causes division, not all the division we feel is due to sin; it was there before sin.

We cannot simply identify matter with sin and spirit with goodness, because sin affected both matter (it is the cause of sickness and death, for example) and spirit (it makes us proud, it weakens our will, and darkens our understanding).

Some of the struggles each one of us experiences are due simply to the fact that we are made of matter as well as spirit. Our material nature will always be blind to spiritual things, our instincts of self-preservation and security will always resist the desires of our spirit to trust God. It's just their nature.

We would perhaps wish it were not so. We wish we were unlimited in our capacities, but we can't be free from needing a few meals a day, or from needing sleep. When there's an emergency and you have to work, and a day goes by and two and your body just can't do any more, you need to rest, you've got to eat. Look at the pictures of rescue workers after a disaster and you can see it on their faces. Their spirit wants to push on, but their bodies are exhausted. We're made of the dust of the earth, we're not angels. We have bodies into which our spirit has been breathed, forming a unity that is at the same time a source of tension.

And on top of that natural tension, there is the complication of sin. We have to remember this or we will be confused and easily disheartened. We will also have false expectations as regards what we can achieve. We must not forget this simple truth—that to make us, God took the dust of the earth, and that dust speaks of fragility, limitation. And it was into this dust that he *breathed the breath of life*.

5. Is it wrong to feel the tension?

Now, sometimes we think that there's something wrong with us when we feel the tug-of-war between these two elements of which we are made. "How come I've got all of these great idealistic desires, yet also such tremendously deep attachments? How come I know God's will, and yet my feelings don't go along with it? Is there something wrong here if I know that the Cross is the source of life, yet I do not want to suffer? Or if I know eternal life is a reality worth sacrificing everything to achieve, yet I keep on putting off renouncing certain things that satisfy me and seem to make me happy, but which I know may not help me get to the life that matters?"

When we think that to be good we have to feel good, we are forgetting that we are made out of matter and spirit, and our feelings are more a part of the material element in us. They are simply incapable on their own of understanding and accepting the things of the spirit, the reality of the spiritual life. They need to be guided, taught, and at times pushed.

ANOTHER SCRIPTURE READING

"Now, the snake was the most subtle of all the wild animals that Yahweh God had made. It asked the woman, 'Did God really say you were not to eat from any of the trees in the garden?' The woman answered the snake, 'We may eat the fruit of the trees in the garden. But of the fruit of the tree in the middle of the garden God said, You must not eat it, nor touch it, under pain of death.' Then the snake said to the woman, 'No! You will not die! God knows in fact that the day you eat it your eyes will be opened and you will be like gods, knowing good from evil.' The woman saw that the tree was good to eat and pleasing to the eye, and that it was enticing for the wisdom that it could give. So she took some of its fruit and ate it. She also gave some to her husband who was with her, and he ate it."

6. Enter sin

On top of the natural tension there is in us between matter and spirit, we have the added difficulty of having to contend with the weakening effects sin has on both of these. Neither is as it should be.

The experience and mistake of our first parents show us the subtlety of the tempter, his almost hypnotic power (because he plays on their natural weakness to create and for illusion), and they also give us an insight into the order we need to restore in our lives so that we can live as God intended.

7. From tension to disarray

The story of our first parents is very sad and thought-provoking. They knew they came from God, and they owed him everything. He had placed them over all creation. He came every day to spend some time with them. They had to know he loved them; their only experience of God was his pure, gratuitous love. Yet the devil came, and in no time he took care of them, just by planting a seed of doubt. "Maybe you can't really trust God; he is out for himself, he is holding out on you, he is afraid you will be a threat to him."

The power of slander and insinuation!

And then we see something truly interesting happen. The woman looks at the fruit, feels the appeal to her senses (pleasing to her eyes) and also to her spirit (desirable because of the wisdom it would give supposedly), and takes an action based on these attractions rather than on what God had said.

In other words, she felt tension between what her senses told her and what her spirit knew (the luscious fruit was crying out to her senses, "Eat me!"). Her spirit knew God had said not to eat from that tree.

And she also felt a tension between what her limited understanding perceived, goaded on by the doubts sown in her mind by the Tempter (the fantasy of "being like God" cried out to her spirit, "Eat me! Become like God!"), and what God had clearly said: "Do not eat it; it will be your death."

Our first parents lived this tension, and because they did not resolve it properly they passed onto us a human nature in disarray, with both the spirit and the matter weakened.

8. First possible solution

One solution, which our first parents did not follow but which we have to strive to restore (and so we could do so, Christ died for us and gives us his grace), is to maintain at all costs the order that God intended.

Our material instincts are blind. They need light and guidance; it is not always right to give into them. Ask anyone who is on a diet. So the material has to be subjected to the spiritual, or else it is likely to self-destruct.

However, our spirit is limited. Our understanding of what is right and wrong is foggy and in many instances needs further light in order not to make mistakes as regards what we should or should not do. This was the case for our first parents, and it is even more the case for us because our intellect is much weaker than theirs as a consequence of their actions.

So the first way to solve the tension is to start from above—to open the skylight and let in the light so our intellect can see more clearly. And then to choose what our enlightened mind sees is right over the objections of our flesh. We will still feel tension, for whether we are fasting because it is good for our blood pressure and cholesterol to knock off a few pounds or because it is Lent and we want to offer a special sacrifice to Christ in reparation for sin, our physical nature is not going to like it and is going to remind us of its discontent through our hunger pangs.

The lesson from this is that when we resolve the tension, the tension itself does not necessarily disappear. More often than not it continues, but we have made up our mind. The tension is no longer in my will being pulled in two different directions; now it is caused by my material self that takes time to appreciate the benefits and catch up with my spirit. The same thing happens when I don't feel like praying or doing what I have to. I may decide to hit the books, but that doesn't change the fact that the weather outside is perfect for a hike in the woods and I would still love to go. That is just my senses holding onto something that attracts them, but my conscience has told me it is not the best for me. It is unrealistic to expect not to have those feelings, and their presence is not a gauge of our goodness and fervor. What we do is.

9. Second solution
The other solution is to avoid the battle, lower our expectations, and let our appetites rule, be they the material appetites of our spirit, or our self-centered spiritual appetites of pride over what God would want.

We are made of the dust of the earth and the breath of God. We find a tension between the two, and we simply say, "Let's forget about the breath of God; I'm just earth, like everybody else." I don't have to tell you how common this solution is, or how inviting. It is common precisely because it is so enticing both to our senses and to our spiritual pride and independence.

CONCLUSIONS

1. Be like God.

The tempter led our first parents to be like God by taking God, his light and his law, out of their lives. We are tempted in the same way. Society is tempted in the same way as well. The fruits in our first parents, in us, and in every society that has tried to do this, are consistent: Disarray.

There is another way to be like God—God's way, Mary's way. And how different are the fruits!

We can be like God by opening our lives to him and letting him work in us. Mary did not understand all God's plan, but she let him work, and because she did what he wanted, she did exactly what she would have done if she were God. Her actions, because of her obedience, had all the power of God's wisdom. She was truly "like God."

We are called to be like God by *breathing the breath of his life* into *the dust* of our daily activities. If it is going to a movie, I will make my choice based on what God would want, not on my curiosity, passions or the opinions of my friends. How I use my time, what I get involved in, the places I go, the people I hang out with, what I study, my moral choices... everything. "I do want to win an Oscar but, no, I will not act in that kind of a movie." "Yes, I am your friend, but if that's what you're going to do, count me out."

Especially in my life-defining decisions, when it is a question of choosing one path or another, of responding to a vocation or not, *breathe the breath of God* into your life. Make it come alive with the wisdom and the power of God. Gain light from your faith. Base your actions on your faith.

2. Do not fear the struggle.

We tend to think there is something wrong when we have to struggle. The only place everything will be fine effortlessly will be in heaven, so we need to adjust our thinking. Far from being a bad sign, struggle is usually a good one, for it means we are imposing the proper order in our life, we are not just "going with the flow," we are giving its place to the spirit.

COLLOQUIES

Take some time to speak now with Christ. He has his own experience of the limitations of his human nature, and his own experience of struggle that we will meditate on later in our retreat.

For now, take your struggle to him. Speak to him of your desires and hopes, and also about your disappointments and struggles.

In his presence, relive spiritually the moment of your creation, in which he *breathed into you the breath of life.*

Thank him.

Reflect back on our first parents and their mistake. See how it applies to you, and ask for his help to see what you have to change in your approach.

Made to Love, Therefore Free
GN 1:26-28

ENTERING INTO THE PRESENCE OF GOD

Lord Jesus, on this retreat I am trying to open the doors of my life to you so you can come in, walk around freely, and tell me what needs care and changing, for you are my Lord, the giver of life.

My faith in you tells me who I really am—your creature—and

who you are as you knock at my door—my Creator, the one who gave me everything. I won't pretend to be the king and lord of my castle; I won't treat you as a beggar on my doorstep. You said, "If you knew who it is who is asking you for a drink, you would ask him and he would give you water that will last forever." I am truly the poor man, needing your grace.

I place my trust in you. I know that with your help I will find and live your plan when you made me out of matter and spirit. I hope in this meditation to discover more deeply your gift and your plan for me.

I love you, and I thank **you** once more for the wonderful gift of my life. I thank you for all that that exists, for everything came from your hands.

Let your Spirit lead me in this meditation as I ask you why you made me, what you had in mind. Knowing this, I will be better able to use your gifts well.

SCRIPTURE PASSAGE

"God said, 'Let us make man in our own image, in the likeness of ourselves, and let them be masters of the fish of the sea, the birds of heaven, the cattle, all the wild animals and all the creatures that creep along the ground.' God created man in the image of himself, in the image of God he created him, male and female he created them. God blessed them, saying to them, 'Be fruitful, multiply, fill the earth and subdue it. Be masters of the fish of the sea, the birds of heaven and all the living creatures that move on earth.'"

EXPLORE THE MEANING
AND MESSAGES OF THE PASSAGE
1. Who is God?

In this passage God reveals what he had in mind when he created us, telling us he chose to make us *in his own image and likeness*. This is a mysterious expression, for God is an invisible Spirit without external form or figure, so what does *in his likeness* mean? What can it mean? What is God like?

We have to depend on God himself to give us an answer, because "no one has seen God. Only the Son who came down from heaven has seen him." So we need to turn to what the Son has shown us about God, and our search takes us to another passage of Scripture, written with the aid of the Holy Spirit after God's revelation in Christ was complete, namely the Apostle John's first letter.

Twice over in this letter John says, "God is love" (1 Jn 4:8, 16). This is as close to a definition as we can get, and it summarizes all God revealed about himself throughout sacred history.

2. God's love

John doesn't simply say God is love, he also gives us the proof. He tells us how we can be sure. "This is the revelation of God's love for us, that God sent his only Son into the world that we might have life through him. Love consists in this: it is not we who loved God, but God loved us and sent his Son to expiate our sins" (1Jn 3:9-10).

John tells us that the sign that God is love and that we are the objects of his love is the sacrifice he was willing to make for our benefit by sending his Son to die and save us from our sins. God did this not in answer to anything we did to please him, but on his own initiative. More startling still, as St Paul points our, he did this while we were "still his enemies." We know he is love because what he did was not easy, and it was not done to serve himself. He did it for us and for our benefit alone.

3. We are made to love

If God created us to be like him, and if he is love, he made us *to love*.

The rest of creation reflects his majesty, power, and intelligence, from subatomic particles to the galaxies and everything in between;

we see it in the instincts of the animals and the ordering of the seasons. But this was not enough. God wanted there to be one creature in his material creation that would be like him, that would be moved not by the blind programming of instincts or the physical and chemical laws of nature, but by what moves God himself, what he himself is, love.

If we don't understand we were made for love, we will not use God's gifts properly, and we will not be fit to be masters over the rest of creation.

Among the gifts God gave us, some he gave particularly, specifically in order to equip us to love. Without them we would not be able to love. He gave us the rest so that we would show our love in the way we use them. Our lives will wander rudderless unless they are built around love and are an expression of love.

So God breathed into us the breath of his life, his "spirit," so that we would live the same life as he, so that we would be his image and likeness, so that we would be able to love. Our spirit is a reflection of his, and it expresses itself in our understanding and free will.

4. Free, in order to love

We value our freedom instinctively. What we do freely defines who we are, and we know that what a man does in the privacy of his own quarters tells us more about him than what he does in public. The types of books he reads on his own tell us more about who he really is and his true interests than the required list of readings for a course he is taking. We know that a "goodness" that is imposed is empty. It may be the right action, but there is still something lacking to it for it to be something truly good and beautiful.

Because of the real importance of freedom to us for our fulfillment as persons, we sometimes think it is the supreme value. "As long as nobody is forcing you" everything and anything is okay. We have no further comment if we call into question another person's actions and get the answer, "But it's my free choice; it's what I want to do." It seems to justify any action.

That, however, is to forget that we are made in the image and likeness of God, who is love.

We know God is free, but we know he is love because he freely gave his life for us. Freedom is made for love, and what we freely choose shows what we love, be it ourselves, our neighbor, God, or whatever.

And the importance of freedom lays in the fact that without freedom there can be no true love. God made us free so we could love. Freedom is a necessary means, but love is the point of our life. And freedom on its own, if it is not understood as a condition to love and is not put at the service of love (or if it is placed at the service of the false "love" which is self-centered) is destructive.

So God gives us the gift of freedom because he wants us to be able to love, and the fact that God made us in order to love explains why he made us free. God made us free for something greater than freedom. He made us to be like himself, to be able to give ourselves like he gives himself.

5. Love well, not blindly

In God's plan, love was not meant to be blind. Jesus loved us and gave himself up for us, not because he had any false illusions about us (he himself knew what was in the heart of man) but because he valued us, he knew the value of an immortal soul and he wanted us to be saved.

Our love is not meant to be blind either. God reproaches those who misused their free choice and chased after false gods. He reproached the foolish rich man who hoarded his riches: "Fool! This very night the demand will be made for your soul; and this hoard of yours, whose will it be then?" He was blinded by his possessions and made a bad choice. So God, along with our freedom and as a guide for our freedom gave us another gift, our intelligence and understanding. He expects us to choose wisely what we love, not to be foolish, for not all things are of the same value.

But it doesn't stop there. Our human intelligence alone is prone

51

to error, and even more so after original sin, so God gave us on top of our human intelligence the gift of faith. Our faith gives us access to the truth of things as seen by God, who alone is Truth itself. We learn the truth from him, through his sacrament of salvation which is the Church, especially in those areas our human reason alone is insufficient. "Set your hearts on his kingdom" (Lk 12:31).

When Jesus speaks about choosing the Kingdom of God above all else, he puts it in an interesting and revealing way. He says, "Set your hearts on his kingdom."

We tend to say, *"Follow your heart."* Jesus says, *"Set your heart."* Love in Christ's mind is a decision, not a feeling. Our heart is powerful, it draws what we are with it, but Jesus tells us we must choose what we are going to focus our heart on. We must choose what we are going to love. He tells us to discriminate: some things are worthy of our love, others are not.

The context in which he uses this phrase, *set your heart*, is the parable we referred to above. He tells the story of a man who had such a bumper crop that he tore down his old barns and built bigger and better ones for all he had and then said, "My soul, you have plenty of good things laid by for many years to come; take things easy, eat, drink, have a good time." But that night he died, so what was the use of all he had? So Jesus tells us to set our hearts on the things that last instead of focusing on those that don't. In Jesus' mind, we decide what we are going to love.

In other words, love is a free act, and because it is, we are responsible for its exercise. We have to be wise in what we choose to love, for if we set our hearts on the wrong things we will never be happy as God intended us to be.

If he made us simply to be free, it would not matter how we use our freedom; it would be perfectly acceptable at the end of my life to say, "Since you wanted me to be free, I decided to become an expert at computer fraud." But we all know that doesn't work.

We really have things together only when we give things the same importance God does, and we set our hearts on those that have real value, without getting carried away by appearances. This is what makes us truly human. Everything else is just a camouflaged slavery, because what is freedom? Is it being able to follow your whims? Is a person free when he's faced with a fifth of whiskey and can't say no to it? Or is he free when he can?

6. The paradox of love

When you love, you freely give yourself. But when you freely give yourself in love, you are no longer "free"! A married man is not "free" to date; indeed, he may not even be "free" to pursue his favorite hobbies because his family needs him at home and not on the golf course.

Nevertheless, even though this is quite obvious, it's amazing to realize that deep down most of us don't really seem to believe it, at least not enough for it to change the way we live.

7. A new type of love

When we hear the word "love," we tend immediately to think of human love, which is very easy for us to imagine. The connection is immediate, especially when the Scripture we are reflecting on says that "God created man in the image of himself [love] …male and female he created them." However, Christ shows us a new type of love that can really only be understood when we look at his example.

Christ was the *image and likeness* of God on two accounts: he was the only Son of God, and he was the Perfect Man. Yet even though Christ was a man, and love is essential to who he was as God and Man, he didn't marry; he didn't have a family. However, there is no doubt that he loved. "He loved his own who were in the world and he loved them to the end." And we have the Cross and the Eucharist to prove it. Each one of us personally has his pardon to prove it.

Christ's capacity to love was not expressed in the exclusive love of a man for his wife and his dedication to his family, but in giving himself up so we could have life through his sacrifice; it showed itself through his mercy, "as he had pity on the crowds for they were like sheep without a shepherd." So, when God himself came in human form the love he lived was shown in the way he gave himself for us, to redeem us from our sins.

In Christ, the word "love" acquires a new meaning and a new depth. Even our human love is transformed by the example of authentic love that Christ lived, a spiritual love that expresses itself in service and giving one's life. That's why our Christian understanding of marriage and the family is so different from the secular one, as St. Paul explained to the Ephesians, and it explains why in a spontaneous and constant manner throughout the history of Christianity, right from the very first Christian communities many men and women were called to the exclusive service of the Lord in virginity and joyful celibacy.

8. Freedom, love, and vocation

It often happens that when we're trying to find our way and our calling in life, we almost want God to go back on his word and take away our freedom. It's as if we want him to come straight out and force us into what he wants us to do. We almost borrow the words of the Jews to Jesus, "How much longer are you going to keep us in suspense?... tell us openly."

It is actually easier at times not to be free and therefore not to have to love. And so we ask for signs that are overwhelming enough to take away all our doubts, signs that we cannot possibly overlook or contradict. "Give me no other option, and I'll follow you." But that is never God's way. God is love. He made you in his image.

God is love, and he gives us the gift of freedom so we can be like him and give our love freely. Only when he leaves us free can he ask us, "Do you love me?" Only when he leaves us our freedom can we answer, "Yes, Lord, I love you."

Christ says to us: "Will you love me... freely? When you have a choice of lifestyles, will you choose to live like my disciple? When your friends and opinion polls say one thing, and I say another, which will you pick? When 'everyone is doing it' and you know 'it' is not my way, which will you choose? When there are many ways of seeking happiness, will you seek my ways? Are you capable of giving yourself freely, as I gave myself for you?"

CONCLUSIONS

God made us to be like him, and he is love. So our love could be authentic, he made us free. So we could love well and love rightly, he gave us the light of reason and the gift of faith.

Christ shows us a new path of love, the redeeming sacrifice of oneself for one's neighbor.

COLLOQUIES

Take time to go back over the main points of the meditation. Go back to those points that caught your attention as you worked through them and spend some time on them, for these are usually the ones God most wants us to listen to and apply in our lives. But don't go back over them in the form of an abstract reflection. Chew on them in conversation with Christ.

Thank our Lord for his gifts.

Thank him for making you free, because thanks to this gift your love will never a prisoner of necessity; you will be able to renew it every day. It can be as fresh years from now as it is today. Since you are free, your love can be as real and fresh in times of trial as in times of ease.

Thank him for the gift of reason, and for enlightening it with the gift of faith.

◈ ◈ ◈

How Have I Used God's Gifts?

LUKE 15:11-32

WHERE WE ARE IN OUR RETREAT

We come from God. We are made by him out of matter and spirit in an individual act of creating love. And he made us in his image, like himself. He gave us his breath of understanding and freedom so we could love, and love well.

Now, in the presence of and with the help of Christ we are going to examine the actual use we have made of these splendid, God-given gifts: the gift of life, the gift of our ability to know God, the gift of our intelligence, the gift of our freedom, and the gift of our love. What have we done with them?

We will do this examination using a parable that Christ told about two sons and their father. The attitude of each of the sons has much to tell us, and it does not take much for us to discover that Jesus in the process gives us a thorough lesson on what sin is, the fruit of sin, and how to overcome it.

ENTERING INTO THE PRESENCE OF GOD

Once more I am here in your presence, Lord, to continue my conversation with you, to continue opening my heart to the light and guidance of your Word in this retreat. I ask you to keep telling me the truth about myself, and to give me the humility to accept it.

I renew my faith in your presence. I know you are here before me in all that you are, body and blood, soul and divinity, true God and true man. I believe that you speak to me through the words of your Scripture. I believe that you speak to me in the depth of my heart through the presence and the voice of the Holy Spirit. I believe that you use human words to provoke the thoughts that you want me to pay attention to. You have shown me that you made me to love, and you gave me the gift of freedom so I could love.

I come in confidence and trust, because I know I am not here to do what I want, but to discover what you want. I know how different your ways are from those of the world that does not know or accept you. I trust in your grace to open my mind and change my heart to understand and love as you understand and love.

I especially desire to have my love renewed, so as to put you at the center of my life. I want to use my freedom to make the choice of love, *to love you above all things and my neighbor as myself.* I freely choose to love and to seek only those things that are good, only those things that are of lasting benefit to myself and to my neighbor. Purify my love so I will love in a Christian way.

I realize in your presence that I am just **your** creature and powerless. All my desires to do good will come to nothing without your grace. I know I have not always loved as I should. Thank you for your patience and for revisiting me so often.

Mary, stay close to me and teach me.

SCRIPTURE PASSAGE:
THE YOUNGER SON AND HIS FATHER

"There was a man who had two sons. The younger one said to his father, 'Father, let me have the share of the estate that will come to me.' So, the father divided the property between them and a few days later the son gathered together everything that he had and left for a distant country where he squandered his money on a life of debauchery.

"And when he had spent it all, that country experienced a severe famine. And now he began to feel the pinch. So he hired himself out to one of the local inhabitants who put him on his farm to feed the pigs. And he would have willingly filled himself with the husks that the pigs were eating, but no one would let him have them. Then he came to his senses and he said, 'How many of my father's hired men have all the food that they want and more, while here I am dying of hunger? I will leave this place and I will go to my father, and I will say, Father, I have sinned against Heaven and against you, I no longer deserve to be one of your sons, so just treat me as one of your hired men.' So, he left that place and went back to his father.

"While he was still a long way off, his father saw him and was moved with pity. He ran to the boy, clasped him in his hands and kissed him. And the son said, 'Father, I have sinned against Heaven and against you. I no longer deserve to be called your son.' But the father said to his servants, 'Quick, bring out the best robe and put it on him, put a ring on his finger and sandals on his feet. Bring the calf we have been fattening and kill it. We will celebrate by having a feast. Because this son of mine was dead and has come back to life, he was lost and is found.' And they began to celebrate."

SCRIPTURE PASSAGE:
THE ELDER SON AND HIS FATHER

"The elder son was out in the fields and on his way back he drew near to the house and he could hear music and dancing. Calling one of the servants he asked what this was all about, and the servant told him, 'Your brother has come, and your father has killed the fatted calf because he has come back safe and sound,' and he was angry and refused to go in. So his father came out and began to urge him to come in. But he retorted to his father, 'All these years I have slaved for you and never once disobeyed any orders of yours, but you never gave me so much as a kid goat for me to

celebrate with my friends. But for this son of yours, when he comes back after swallowing all of your property, he and his loose women, you killed a calf you have been fattening.' And the father said, 'My son, you are with me always, and all I have is yours. But it was only right that we would celebrate and rejoice, because your brother here was dead and has come to life, he was lost and is found.'"

EXPLORE THE MEANING
AND MESSAGES OF THE PASSAGE
1. The younger son's insolence

We have here a young man whose father is obviously very successful, with a thriving farm, laborers, and servants. The sons know each will get a part when their father dies. But the younger son has his own plans and is rather impatient to get on with them. To do so, he gives his father a huge slap in the face. We are so used to hearing the parable that it has lost all its shock value, so let's rephrase it: "Father, I can't wait for you to die so as to get my hands on your money, so give it to me now, and let's get out of each other's life."

So he got his money and left home to do with it what he wanted, certainly not things his father would approve of. At least he had the sensitivity to go far away to do it.

We have here the clash of two ideas of how to live life. The son has no time for his father's opinion, and he sets out for a "distant country."

But the money he did it with was a gift came from his father. The son tells the father he has no time for him, all he wants is the money; he takes the gift and does with it what he wants.

It is not hard to see in Jesus' words his description of sin, and to picture as he wants us to God's heartbreak as he watches us take the gifts he lavished upon us with so much love (life, freedom) and walk away, full of our own "much better" ideas as to how to use them, with no time for him, his love, or his wisdom... his sorrow at us wanting to "be like God" on our own terms.

2. The younger son learns reality

The young man gives himself to every whim and pleasure, enjoying his artificial friends who love him as long as the next round is on him. Jesus cuts right to the point: material goods do not last forever. A severe famine hits, and the son "begins to feel the pinch." By that time all his money is gone, and with it his friends, too.

So what he thought was lasting, what he thought was a sure thing, the trust he put in his possessions, and the trust he put in people evaporated before his very eyes. He discovers that if you "put your faith in men," as the psalm says, you'll "be accursed," disappointed, the unhappiest of men. And that's what he had done. What good now are all the pleasures, all the riches, all the friends he thought he had? So his plans begin to unravel, because he had sought in material things what they cannot give.

Think about what he would have answered if you had asked him when he was setting out on his journey, "Do you want loneliness? Do you want poverty? Do you want misery? Do you want to be a slave?" Why, that is what he was running away from. He didn't want poverty, because he made sure to have saddlebags of his father's money before he started off. He didn't want suffering, because he was going away to seek all the pleasures of the world. He didn't want loneliness, because he was going to buy friends for himself. He didn't want slavery, for he was escaping from his father. And yet here we have him with his plans totally unraveled. He used his freedom unwisely; he placed his trust in what was passing, hoping it would give him lasting pleasure, and he was mistaken. A bitter pill to swallow!

Jesus is warning us, and asking us to examine our own experience to see that the fruits of sin are very different from the Tempter's promises, as our first parents found out.

3. Rock bottom

The young man is treated worse than an animal. He was so hungry that he wanted to eat the scraps that were fed to the pigs, but *no one would let him have them.* To the owner, it was more important to feed the pigs than him. He is useful to take care of the pigs, but they come first. He would have to fight with the pigs for food when nobody was looking.

4. Two pivotal moments
Thinking Straight

Jesus says, "He came to his senses." This is crucial. He began to think. He started to use his mind to give things their proper value. Sinning is following a false perception of reality. There is always something irrational about sin. Now he is coming around; he is thinking. Life in his present condition is worse than what he had with his father. "Even the servants at my father's house have food on the table, plenty of food on the table, what am I doing here?"

And this leads to a decision: "I'll go back to my father and admit that I have sinned against heaven and against him. Maybe he'll let me back as one of his servants." He knows he hasn't behaved as a son and so does not deserve to be accepted back as one. He is being honest and objective about his behavior.

True conversion involves a hard look at reality—not liking what you see and knowing there's got to be something better. Conversion cannot be simply an emotional reaction; it has to be a readjustment of our criteria.

Following Through

"So he left the place and went back to his father." Easier said than done, but conversion is not complete until it becomes action.

Too often we take the first step of recognizing our sin, but then we do not move. We go to the same parties, keep the same friends, we don't ever make time for prayer. Not this young man. He has a lesson for us. He bites the bullet, he gets up, steps out of his self-pity, he gets moving.

5. Returning home, no easy thing

To go back to his father he had to be willing to say, "Everything I did was wrong; you were right." To go back to his father he had to expose himself to the ridicule of his older brother. How would the servants treat him? If he behaved as he did with his father, just imagine how he treated the servants. And now he was going to be one of them.

A Necessary Difficulty

Every step of the way back must have been a struggle, since it was a long journey from that *distant land*, and he was on foot. Every step of the way he must have thought of giving up; he was weak, exhausted, famished… it was bad with the pigs, but at least there were a few crumbs for him, and he knew what to expect. He *went back to his father*. What great inner strength! How many times have we gotten up to go back but not quite made it because the road was long and difficult, because the temptations were still there….

Conversion is a difficult, heroic road.

Fruitful Difficulty

The long and difficult journey changed him.

When he set out at the beginning of his conversion, he was thinking of himself. "I'm hungry, my father's servants are treated better than this, I'm going back to see if I can be accepted as a servant, because at least I want to eat." The confession of what he did wrong still seems to be a means to an end—food. "Imperfect contrition" is the technical term for this.

However, as he makes his long journey and rehearses the words over and over in his mind they begin sink into his heart. "I really am not worthy to be called his son; just look at what I did! I remember the look of sadness on his face, and how I despised him as I rode away. Now I can imagine how he felt…." He understands this to such a degree that when his father runs out and embraces him and it is obvious he has been pardoned, he still has to say to his father, "I'm not worthy to be called your son; I've sinned against heaven and against you."

He is no longer at the center. He is sorry now, not because he is hungry and paying the price of his sin, but because of what he did to his father, because of how he hurt him.

That is why the journey of conversion is long and difficult, because it is not complete with the first step. God wants to make us his sons again, and to be truly his sons we have to realize what an unmerited gift it is to be forgiven and become his sons again.

We need to progress to "perfect contrition," which does not focus on the bad consequences of our sins for us but on the hurt we cause God—because he deserves our love above all else.

6. The false goodness of the second son

Jesus paints a picture of the other son. On the surface he looks like the perfect son, all that his younger brother was not. He remained close to his father. He never took off on him. He was hardworking, last in from the fields, as we see in Jesus' story. He never asked for anything special.

However, as he reveals himself in his actions and words we discover there is much that he too needs to change.

The Thoughts of His Heart Laid Bare

He comes home to find that the younger brother has returned, and their father is throwing a party for him. And we suddenly see how different he was from his father—how different his heart was despite living in the same house, sharing the same table, their frequent conversations. He does not share his father's heart. He has not learned to love as his father. He does not understand his love.

And look at how he describes his work for his father that on the surface seemed so faithful and full of love: "All these years I have slaved for you." Where is the friendship, love, and trust? The father has to remind him, because he seems to doubt it: "Son, you are with me always, and all that I have is yours." Was he afraid his father would now make him share it with his younger brother?

And on top of this, he accuses his father; he tells him that he is neither fair nor just. "How come you killed the fatted calf for him and you never did for me? Is that fair treatment?" It is not hard to picture him, voice raised, veins popping, finger stabbing at his father....

Why was there no joy that his brother had been saved? He was thinking only of himself, and that didn't allow him to love as his father loved. And what did one fatted calf matter, if his father told him, "All that is mine is yours?" This son thinks it is his father who has to change, not himself.

The Thoughts of Our Hearts

Sometimes we think that because we have no great, obvious sins, we are special and don't need to change. Maybe our parents have gone to great lengths to protect us from what could have gone wrong in our lives, and we think that because of that, because we are "practicing Catholics," because we know our catechism and belong to some Church group, everything is fine. Worse still, maybe we feel we can sit in judgment of others.

Jesus invites us to look into our hearts. Do we find presumption, judgmentalism, pride, superiority? Are we stingy, miserly with the gifts God gave us? Do we just want to go on living our comfortable life, and when God asks us to be as generous as he is, to give up our own plans and security and serve others, do we answer him, "All these years I have slaved for you..." Do we view the graces and care he has lavished on us as a burden?

If we have been blessed by God, we should be more generous, not less. God's blessings are not a passport to comfort, but to service.

7. A self-examination

There is a bit of both sons in each and all of us.

We have taken God's gift, the great gift of freedom, and used it to love what we shouldn't have, some to a greater degree than others. We have used our reason badly and given passing things a value they do not have, loving them with a love that only God should command.

Even if we left him and have now come back, there is part of us that reflects the son who stayed with his father, but still doesn't understand, think, love, and react as he does. The part of us that registers the burden and the drudgery and has forgotten the love... the part that begrudges him his invitation, that feels it is an imposition... the part that never stops to realize how much happier and at peace the father is in his love than his son is in his envy... the part that is like the workers sent out early in the fields who complain because the master is generous with the latecomers (cf. Mt 20, 1-15).

8. The father

Jesus is describing his heavenly Father to us in this man that never forgot his younger son. Despite the sting of his son's insult and rejection, the father waited and hoped. He was the first to spot him even at a distance. The last one to lose hope in us is God.

When we recognize our weakness is when he lifts us up and makes us his sons. After the miraculous catch of fish, Peter throws himself at the feet of Christ saying, "Lord, depart from me because I am a sinful man." Instead of sending him away, Jesus says, "You are going to be a fisher of men" (cf. Lk. 5,4-10). When Peter realizes he is sinful, the door really opens between Christ and himself, and Christ can make him what he should be.

CONCLUSIONS

We have much to ask God's pardon for. This story that Christ told is really about us. Look at the picture of yourself. Face your shortcomings sincerely. Look at reality, how you have used God's gift of freedom, what you love, the goals you pursue.

Choose the path home. Travel the long distance that lies between you and the father, even if you are the son who remained at home.

Renew your trust. The father always loves.

Renew your gratitude.

Renew your love. God has called each one of us to be his apostles in the world, and we need to love others as God has loved us. Do I pardon, love, pray for my enemies and those who do so much damage to the Church? Am I prepared to give my life for them?

COLLOQUIES

Lord Jesus, you are so patient. No matter how difficult the journey is, let me always be convinced that you are there with me, waiting to embrace me. Let me learn not to be so self-absorbed so I can love as you love and deserve to be loved.

Grant me the grace, grant me the honesty, and grant me the strength to turn my life around and to use your gifts as you intended me to.

Let me not be afraid to imitate my Father.

Reconciliation with God: The Sacrament of Confession

This is a very good moment in your retreat to take time to examine your conscience and prepare a good confession.

Take the attitudes of the two sons as a basis and a point of reference, examine in more depth than usual your love for Christ and your failings, confess your sins with total openness and humility to Christ in the sacrament, and receive his pardon.

This will help you remove any attachments you may have to what is not Christ and his will, and it will make it easier to overcome the obstacles you face to your growth in Christ. His grace will be more unhindered in its action, and you will be freer to love him more sincerely.

If you have any hesitation, you can more easily overcome it by remembering that you are going to the loving father, who is already running to embrace his humbled son, anxious to reclothe him with the robe of his grace and to restore his gifts to him.

Some retreatants find it very helpful to make an examination of their whole life, or a major part of it, and then to make what is called a general confession of that larger period of their life.

PART II

After examining our lives in the light of the parable of the prodigal son and recognizing our shortcomings in the way we use God's gift of freedom, we will begin the reconstruction of our lives centered on Jesus' example.

He was true man. He had a human understanding and a human will as well as the divine understanding and will that were his as Son of God.

We will let our souls be enlightened by looking at how he used these gifts of understanding and freedom. We will let his example inspire and transform us. We will ask for his grace to follow him and try to live like him.

Tried and Tested

MATTHEW 4:1-11

ENTERING INTO THE PRESENCE OF GOD

Lord Jesus, once more I am here in your presence to spend some time with you, to pray, to speak to you, but above all to listen to you, to hear the words you speak to me through your Gospel—to listen to them attentively and to receive them into my life with the help of your Holy Spirit.

I believe you are present here in the Eucharist, like the patient father awaiting the return of his son. I know there is something special, some special light you wish to give me in this meditation. Open the eyes of my mind, the eyes of my soul, to your word and grace. Make me docile to the work of the Holy Spirit as I contemplate your example.

Looking at the story of the two sons, I have discovered so many weaknesses in my life, so much "love" centered on me instead of you. Although weighed down by the awareness of my faults, I come to you with hope in your grace and trust in your love. I know I will find in your example the way to follow and the *truth* that gives *life*.

I come to this meditation with love in my heart, but a love still weak and wavering, distracted by other "loves." I come to learn from your steadfast love in your time of trial; I come to learn from your example. I am a sinner, yet I long to be your faithful servant.

I thank you for this new opportunity and this new sign of your love that you show me by having me with you on this retreat today, spending all your time with me.

Mary, guide me to Christ. You were *full of Grace, faithful Virgin.* Help me serve him as faithfully.

SCRIPTURE PASSAGE

"Then Jesus was led by the Spirit out into the desert to be put to the test by the devil. He fasted for forty days and forty nights after which he was hungry. And the tester came and said to him, 'If you are the Son of God tell these stones to turn into loaves.' But he replied, 'Scripture says man lives not on bread alone but on every word that comes from the mouth of God.' The devil then took him to the Holy City and stood him on the parapet of the Temple. 'If you are the Son of God,' he said, 'Throw yourself down, for Scripture says, He has given his angels order about you and they will carry you in their arms if you trip over a stone.' Jesus said to him, 'Scripture also says, Do not put the Lord your God to test.' Next, taking him to a very high mountain the devil showed him all the kingdoms of the world in their splendor and he said to him, 'I will give you all these if you fall at my feet and give homage.' Then Jesus replied, 'Away with you, Satan, for Scripture says, The Lord your God is the one to whom you must do homage and him alone must you serve.' Then the devil left him and suddenly angels appeared and looked after him."

And St Luke's ending in chapter 4, verse 13, says, *"Having exhausted every way of putting him to the test, the devil left him until the opportune moment."* In other words, he didn't leave him completely in peace. This devil had other plans and was going to come back later on to carry them out.

EXPLORE THE MEANING
AND MESSAGES OF THE PASSAGE

A Special Passage

There is no one else present but Jesus, the Tempter, and the angels. So news of it had to have come from Jesus' own lips. This means that

Jesus specifically wanted his followers to know that he was tempted, what the temptations were, and what the outcome was.

1. Why?

What provoked Jesus one day to turn to his apostles and say, "Look, do you know what happened to me in the desert?" and go on to tell them the whole story? Nothing is by chance in Jesus' life, so we know for sure that one day he felt they needed to know this, and that we need to know it too.

We tend to think that everything was very simple and straightforward for the apostles, right? Sure, they had their ups and downs, but with Jesus there to turn to, how could there be problems? But what does Jesus telling his apostles about his encounter with the devil hint at? He was addressing their present and future temptations.

Years later, St. Peter in his letters described the devil as "a marauding lion, seeking someone to devour." A spine-chilling description—a picture of sleepless men drawing close around a campfire, seeking comfort and protection in numbers, as they listen in huddled and fearful silence to the roars and ceaseless padding of the hungry, *marauding lion*, sniffing and circling in the darkness about them.

2. The disciples' trials

Peter was talking from experience. He had been put to the test by the devil and had not done too well. Tempted to pride and superiority at the Last Supper, he gave in; tempted to betrayal a few hours later, he swore he never knew Jesus. Was that his first encounter with the devil? Jesus said, "Satan has sought you, but I have prayed for you so that once you turn back you will confirm your brothers in the faith."

The apostles must have had many down days on the long and dusty roads of Palestine. Tired and thirsty, thrown out of the Samaritan villages, harassed by the Pharisees ("Your Master doesn't pay the temple tax"; "He casts out demons by the power of the prince of demons"; "See, he breaks the Sabbath"; "He is not educated"; "No prophet ever came from where he's from")—the barrage became ceaseless. We don't think enough about the difficulties the apostles had, the times it seemed temptingly easy just to go back and fish again and have some peace. Especially when Jesus began to speak of death on a cross, and a grain of wheat falling into the ground and dying.... John and James had to accept not to seek the first places, Simon the Zealot had to digest the words, "Love your enemies." Every one of them "had to enter by the narrow gate."

One day, Jesus found it necessary to tell them about the devil and his tactics, and also about his limitations—how he can be stopped, although he never gives up and keeps coming back. He told them about one of his encounters with the devil, and in the process gave us a lesson in how to use the Father's gifts of love and freedom.

And this seemed so important and helpful to the apostles that they made sure to tell the story to all Jesus' followers, and so it has reached you and me.

3. Temptations have their place

What did Jesus go out to the desert for? We tend to answer "to fast and pray." St. Matthew says something totally different: "Jesus was led by the Spirit out into the desert to be put to the test by the devil." Then Scripture says, "He fasted for forty days and forty nights," almost as if to say that the explanation of his prayer and fasting was to be found in the purpose of his going out; i.e., to be tempted.

The Father's Spirit led Jesus into the desert to be tempted. It was God's plan that he be put to the test. And to meet that testing, Jesus fasted and prayed.

So the temptations we face in life can have a purpose. God can turn them to good. Gold has to be tested in the fire. What is not gold has to be burned off so that only pure gold will remain. Remember when he spoke about the seed that had no roots, that "in times of trial fell away"? Trial and testing is necessary. Jesus faced it, and Jesus prevailed.

Another Example of Testing

Remember Job?

Job was prosperous and God was proud of him, so Satan says to God, "He's good only because you're treating him well. Let me take away some of his success, and I bet he'll be cursing you before the day is done." God gave the devil some limited power over Job, who then in swift succession lost all his possessions and his children. He was reduced to misery and covered with sores, but he never cursed God. And God gave him back more than before.

We need to test ourselves constantly by seeking greater virtue and greater challenges. And we need to let God test us by allowing what we call "temptations." We cannot rashly expose ourselves to the force of our evil passions and desires, but when God allows it, we can be sure he is always there with his grace to strengthen us.

The first lesson we learn from Jesus is that temptation is not an anomaly in our Christian life; it is part of God's plan.

Especially if God calls you to be his priest, you will have to become like Christ by preparing for trials, and being faithful in them.

Christ's Example
4. The first temptation—food

One day when they really needed to hear it, Jesus says something like: "Trials are necessary. That is how I started. I was sent out to meet the devil, so first I fasted for forty days and forty nights, and only then did the devil come—when I was tired and hungry. So the first thing he said as he pointed to the stones there in the desert smoothed by the wind and sand, almost looking like loaves fresh out of the oven, "Congratulations, you have really done something wonderful, fasting and praying for forty days—amazing! Only the greatest prophets have fasted and prayed for forty days, like Moses on the mountain. You are a Holy Man. Remarkable! Now, why not take a break? If you are the Son of God, you have power to turn these stones into loaves. Do so and eat something; you deserve it. I'm not asking you to abuse your power and have a banquet. Just a piece of bread. I mean, God your Father is not going to begrudge you a piece of bread, is he?"

Jesus' Answer

The devil wants Jesus to focus on his own needs and preferences and to make his choices based on these. Jesus tells the apostles his answer: "The Father's will is...." The devil was trying to get him to shift his point of reference, and he used very human and reasonable arguments to do so, anything to shift Jesus' center of attention away from this bothersome thing called the will of God expressed in the word of God. He didn't start by tempting Jesus to do something bad, just to move the center a little. And Jesus put things right back where they ought to be. "'Man does not live on bread alone, but on every word that comes from the mouth God.' It doesn't matter what my appetites say, it is what God says that matters." Later on in life, he would say when the apostles thought he had been given something to eat, "I have other food to eat... My food is to do the will of the Father."

This is his first answer to this very reasonable and humanly desirable suggestion of the devil.

5. The second temptation—a sign

The devil's reaction is not to go away, but to up the ante. This is what frustrates us about him. We expect temptation to go away after we answer it properly and don't fall, but he only comes back.

We don't know how it happened, but he set Jesus on the parapet of the Temple and said, "So you like the Scriptures... well, consider this:'He will give his Angels orders about you. They will carry you in their arms in case you trip over a stone.' If you believe this and if you are the Son of God, then throw yourself off this parapet. People will see the sign; they will accept you as the Son of God and the Messiah; they will flock to you."

Implied here is the temptation to take a shortcut, to have a better plan than God. Jesus would say later, "When the Son of Man is raised up he will draw all people to himself," and John tells us that he was talking about his crucifixion. The devil is telling him there is an easier way to draw all people to himself.

How come, when the devil tempts us, it always seems to be to the wide and easy road, while God offers the narrow gate and the steep path?

Jesus' Answer

First of all, Jesus doesn't get disheartened that the devil comes on stronger instead of going away .

Second, he doesn't lose his focus. "Scripture also says, Do not put the Lord your God to the test." He refused to contemplate or rationalize anything that was not his Father's will. He cuts the tempter off; he doesn't engage in discussion.

6. The third temptation—compromise

The devil doesn't give up yet. He cannot take no for an answer, so he tries again.

"Next, taking him to a high mountain the devil showed him all the kingdoms of the world and their splendor. And he said to him, 'I will give you all of these if you will follow at my feet and do me homage.'"

Luke puts it like this, "I will give you all this power and their splendor for it has been handed over to me for me to give to anyone I choose. Do homage then to me and it will all be yours." Luke lets us see how daring the devil is. "The world is mine; if you want to conquer it, just ask me. *I can do with them as I choose.*" How tempting it is to do apostolate, to try to change the world by pandering to the reign of sin in the world. *"Kneel down and pay me homage."*

When the devil got our first parents to sin, through their weakness he acquired a power in the world that was not his by right, and he exercises it to the hilt. Check out your own life. He uses it to strip us away from God. Jesus later on calls the devil "the father of lies." He truly is. He exaggerates when he describes his power, and he has no intention of giving it up. He simply wants to co-opt Jesus' saving mission before it even starts.

The devil never walks away. We commit one sin, and he wants a repetition, frequent sin; from frequent sin to a bad habit, from a bad habit to a hardened vice, making us carve out a Grand Canyon that we lose all hope of climbing out of. He had no intentions of turning everything over to Jesus. And yet he made the promise.

Are we surprised that he lies to us, promising us heaven on earth, happiness, and possessions in this life forever?

Jesus' Answer

The brazenness of the claim and the temptation has to have hit Jesus hard, but he doesn't get thrown off balance. He meets the devil's new attempt with resolve.

Again he keeps his focus on his Father's will expressed in the Scriptures. "Away with you, Satan, for Scripture says, the Lord your God is the one to whom you must do homage, and him alone must you serve."

It is so tempting to make our mark in the world by condescending to the world. *"Get down off your cross and we will believe you."* "Give us a Gospel without the cross and we will follow you." He couldn't come down off the cross and still save us, no matter what they said, so he remained faithful. People today say to the Church, "Don't preach this extreme, radical gospel of honesty, marital fidelity, all such things. Condone, don't condemn, and then we'll believe in you." Or, "Don't be so fanatical about obeying the Holy Father. Treat him as one opinion among many; pick and choose, and then we'll be with you all the way." It's a constant temptation to do homage to the world to get it back on a platter.

In our personal lives, we think we can remain at the center and still serve Christ, that we can do homage to ourselves, our ambitions and passions, and still be faithful to him. Christ's answer is the same always; he goes straight to his Father's will – "The Lord your God is the one to whom you must do homage. And him alone you must serve."

Jesus sweeps aside all the sophistry, all the smoke and mirrors— leaving us with the truth.

7. The outcome

The devil left him. Victory.

Luke says, "The devil left him until the opportune moment," because the devil won't give up as long as we live.

Angels appeared and looked after Jesus, like they do for us when we go through temptation. When we persevere through difficult temptations and darkness, no matter how dark and hopeless things seem as we go through them, we always emerge into the light, which is always brighter if we have been faithful.

CONCLUSIONS

Draw your conclusions by comparing yourself to Jesus.

Jesus prepared for temptation by prayer and fasting. In prayer, he familiarized himself with his Father's desire, in prayer he received light, in prayer he renewed his love.

In fasting, he reminded his sinless flesh of its place. He will not ever let it usurp the role of guiding his choices.

During temptation, Jesus uses his mind and memory to recall his Father's wishes. Based on what he knows these are, no matter what the tempter says he makes his decision: to love and follow what his Father wants.

Contrast this with our first parents, whose thought pattern in temptation was, "It is pleasing to the senses... it is desirable for the power it gives."

At no time do we see him looking longingly at the alternative, saying, "If only I could," or questioning his Father's will.

His free choice was totally guided by his love for his Father. The supreme expression of his freedom was to choose the Father's will despite the promptings and, at times vicious attempts of the devil.

COLLOQUIES

Take some moments on your own to reflect and talk directly with Jesus about his experience. As you compare his actions to your own, talk to him; ask him to give you strength.

Let us ask him if temptation overcomes us so easily because we go to meet it unprepared, not having sacrificed, not having prayed.

Let us ask him to take away our fear of resisting temptation, to help us not to give up so easily.

Speak to Jesus who left you this story so you could realize that he understands you, and that he wants you to understand the nature of the call he is giving you—a life, certainly of struggle, but a struggle that he has already shown us how to win, through him, with him, and in him.

Battle in Gethsemane

MK 14:32-42

ENTERING INTO THE PRESENCE OF GOD

Lord, once more I come before you as my retreat progresses. You are placing many thoughts in my soul. Especially, you are revealing to me who you are, what you have given me, your hopes for me, and how rich you are in mercy and forgiveness. You are giving me your living example of how I should live.

I believe that you're really present here in the Eucharist, which is your greatest gift to me. Everything else I can think of (life, qualities, people, possessions) are merely creatures. You are the Eucharist, *the fountain of life* itself. You came as a man, and at times I treat you as if that is all you are. You come under the signs of the Sacrament, and I neglect your presence. I am unworthy to have you as my spiritual food, to be here in your presence.

I come looking for light, strength, and decision. I place all my efforts in your hands. I know that you know what I need, and you wish to give it to me once I ask for it. I hope and trust in you, I want to learn from you to love, to use my freedom to love *to the end*.

Mary, *a sword pierced your heart,* yet you were faithful to the end, *standing near the Cross of Jesus* as he gave his life for us. Help me to take his example into my heart and to act upon it, as you did.

SCRIPTURE PASSAGE

Matthew says, "*He took along Peter and the two sons of Zebedee, and he began to feel sorrow and distress.*"

Now let's continue with Mark.

"Then they came to a place called Gethsemane, and he said to his disciples, 'sit here while I pray. He took with him Peter, James and John, and he began to be troubled and distressed. Then he said to them, 'My soul is sorrowful even to death. Remain here and keep watch.' He advanced a little then fell on the ground and prayed that if it were possible this hour might pass him by. 'Abba Father, all things are possible for you. Take this cup away from me. But not what I will, but what you will.' When he returned he found them asleep and he said to Peter, 'Simon, are you asleep? Could you not keep watch for one hour? Watch and pray that you will not undergo the test. The spirit is willing but the flesh is weak.' Withdrawing again, he prayed saying the same thing. 'Father, all things are possible to you. Take this cup away from me. But not what I will, but what you will.' Then he returned once more where he again found them asleep. They could not keep their eyes open and they did not know what to answer. And he returned a third time and he said to them 'Are you still sleeping and taking your rest? It's enough. The hour has come. Behold the Son of Man has to be handed over to sinners. Get up. Let us go. My betrayer is here at hand.'"

EXPLORE THE MEANING
AND MESSAGES OF THE PASSAGE

1. An extraordinary passage

Like the temptations of Jesus, this passage tells us something real that happened to Jesus that we could never have imagined or made up ourselves. Yet it is so important that every single Gospel includes it, with varying detail and emphasis.

A "Different Jesus"?

Many times during his life they had laid traps for Jesus and sought to take him prisoner or kill him. They never succeeded.

They feared the crowds. On one occasion the armed guards came back with the lamest excuse ever for not taking a suspect into custody: "No one ever spoke like this man!" The disciples were often worried and afraid, but never Jesus. His power was greater than the swords and lances of those guards.

Yet here Jesus is distressed, agitated. We see him battle. He had said, "I and my Father are one… I always do what pleases him… My food is to do my Father's will." Now he cries out and groans, "If is possible, take away this cup from me." And he lets himself get taken prisoner. This time he does not walk through his enemies, as before in Nazareth. An unexpected, new depth to the mystery of Jesus and our redemption is being revealed here before our eyes.

2. The difference with our struggles

We often say the first part of Jesus' prayer, telling God we wish he would ask something else of us. The reason we do is quite simple: we have our passions; we are attached to so many other things that are not God; our love is weak. Our struggles are struggles of rebellion.

Not so with Jesus. His battle was not against disordered passions, because he did not have any. Yet there was a struggle—an enormous struggle that was so deep, so emotional, so passionate, and so prolonged that it lasted several hours. At one point "his sweat became as drops of blood falling to the ground," as Luke tells us.

We can always say when we have to suffer that "we deserved it." There is always some sin to atone for in our lives, so many things we have gotten away with for which we need to be make reparation.

Not so in Jesus.

3. The meaning of the struggle

Let us accept what the Gospel tells us, and without presuming to be able to understand all its implications, let us try to learn from it.

Jesus' human nature did not seek the cross of its own desire. It found the cross repulsive, and it had to be brought into submission in order to accept it.

The power that brought it into submission was not external coercion, but the interior force of love: "Not my will but yours be done." And his love for us: "I lay down my life for my sheep."

Jesus was being asked to do something that on the surface was a total injustice, humanly speaking. He was sinless, and because of this he was being asked to die in the place of the real sinners. He was being asked to undergo the punishment of the unjust precisely because he was innocent, so that the unjust would be saved. He was being asked to give his life for those who would put him to death. And all of us did, because we all sin.

This does not make sense humanly. As a matter of fact, it seems like the opposite of justice. It is something that human nature, even if it is sinless, cannot get enthusiastic about, because in a certain sense it is repugnant.

Jesus' perfect human nature can only accept, can only "process" it by entering a different level, the level of voluntary acceptance of another light, another nature that sees things as they really are, and submitting its human self to that greater light and will.

The form that his love took was obedience to his Father's will. We expect God's will to save us from the cross and suffering, but that is not what Jesus sought or received.

The writer of the Letter to the Hebrews says, "During his life on earth, he offered up prayer and entreaty, with loud cries and with tears, to the one who had the power to save him from death, and, winning a hearing by his reverence, he learnt obedience, Son though he was, through his sufferings; when he had been perfected, he became for all who obey him the source of eternal salvation and was acclaimed by God with the title of high priest of the order of Melchizedek."

4. How Jesus conducts his struggle

First of all, he's open with God in prayer. He does not hide his problem. He says, "Father, everything is possible to you." And very simply he states what he would prefer: "Take away this cup from me."

Then he goes a step farther; he takes the step of love and surrender. He seeks first the kingdom of his Father, knowing that "everything else will be added" to him. "However, not what I will, but what you will."

Why did Christ pray if he already had his mind made up to do the Father's will? Why did he bother to say what his own will was? Because he was the Son, he was totally open and trusting with his Father, he was not ashamed of the limitations of his human nature, perfect though it was. The human heart and the human will of the Son speak.

From this moment on, our prayers are heard differently by God. Even our struggles remind him of his Son, and in all our struggles Christ understands and identifies himself with us. Our prayers never rise to the Father without reminding him of his Son. From these hours of Christ's struggle is born the confidence with which we can turn to God always and say with Christ and in Christ, "The Father always listens to me."

But when we pray, do we let the Father hear once again the voice of the Son who loves him, saying, "Not my will, but yours be done"? Often, this is the major conquest we have to strive for in our prayer, to echo Christ's love and trust in his Father.

There is nothing the Father can ask of us that's more difficult than what Christ has done, or the Father has done in sacrificing his only Son. Only good can come from us putting ourselves in God's hands. Jesus knows: "The Father loves me always."

Jesus didn't just come to tell us, "Look, what Adam and Eve did was wrong. You need to trust the Father. And take it from me, I know heaven. I'm the Son of God. So write this down and do it." No, Jesus "walks the walk." He teaches his lesson by living it.

5. The loneliness of the struggle

Jesus asks his chosen, closest apostles to accompany and pray with him. He asks them to join him in prayer and to watch and pray for themselves too, so that they will not fall into temptation. They sleep. Three times. Jesus knows the time of trial is near for them, he knows the devil is *seeking to devour them*, but his words fall on deaf ears.

Yet Jesus does not give up because he feels alone and abandoned, and the suffering ahead is terrible. He is a Rock of unshakable love.

But will we abandon him too, leaving him to struggle alone? We have the opportunity now to offer him our fidelity, to promise not to leave him on his own, suffering for the world.

6. The power of love

We discover in Jesus a dual love, for the Father and for souls, that is really one. Jesus' identification with his Father's will goes far beyond the materiality of accepting and doing what the Father wants, in this case to suffer and die. He goes on to fully identify himself with the purpose behind his Father's will, in this case to redeem us from our sins. He makes the Father's will and intention his own; there is no separation between his love for his Father's will and his love for us. He loves us because the Father loves us, and as the Father loves us, to the point of laying down his life willingly to save us.

This is the pattern for our love for souls, to try to love them in the same way and to the same degree as Christ loves them, willing to give our very life for them if necessary, and in the process overcoming the limitations and hesitations of our human nature.

7. The outcome

Calm returns. Jesus rises and goes out to meet the betrayer. He does not hide; there is no hesitation, anguish, or fear. He even saves his apostles. As John tells us:

"Knowing everything that was to happen to him, Jesus came forward and said, 'Who are you looking for?' They answered, 'Jesus the Nazarene.' He said, 'I am he.' Now Judas the traitor was standing among them. When Jesus said to them, 'I am he,' they moved back and fell on the ground. He asked them a second time, 'Who are you looking for?' They said, 'Jesus the Nazarene.' Jesus replied, 'I have told you that I am he. If I am the one you are looking for, let these others go.' This was to fulfil the words he had spoken, 'Not one of those you gave me have I lost.'"

CONCLUSIONS

Our own Gethsemane should never take us by surprise. We can't expect that our human nature will always be thrilled and joyous with the demands of our vocation. We can't expect to understand God's plan if we merely stay on the human level. We have to open our lives to faith and love, the light that faith and love give us, and make our decisions based on what we see with the eyes of faith and not with our human vision.

Everything we do is based on this trust in God, on knowing what he is really like, which we find out through what Jesus said and did.

So, trust in God, yes; love for him, yes – but that is not all. We also accept and do his will because we identify with his love for his sheep. The souls I am called to serve must focus my decisions and influence them.

As we strive to see what God wants us to do, let us always affirm our trust in God and our love and commitment to his will.

We have the opportunity to repeat in our own life the same pattern of love and trust in God, going beyond our natural inclinations and overcoming our natural resistance to the sacrifices God asks of us. Will I love God enough to accept his way, to give myself for others?

COLLOQUIES

Take some time to pray. It may help to look at the crucifix. Look at the crucifix and say to Christ in your heart, "This is what you saw coming; this is how much you trusted your Father, enough to go through all this when humanly speaking there was no reason to."

True love seems like madness, the type of love martyrs have.

Lord, here in the Garden you show me the relationship to have with my Father in heaven. "Father, if it's possible, take away this chalice. But your will be done, not mine." I know that if I do what you want, if I put myself totally in your hands, no evil can harm me. With you the greatest trials are a blessing. "To lose my life for the sake of your kingdom is to gain it."

Thank you, Lord, for going through Gethsemane for me. "You are in Gethsemane and on the cross so that when I return from the distant land of sin I will encounter your pardon, not your wrath."

I hear your words to your apostles, "Be with me; pray with me." You say them to me. I will never leave you to struggle alone.

Christ's Four Thirsts
JOHN 19:28

ENTERING INTO THE PRESENCE OF GOD

Lord, I believe in you, and I know that believing in you means accepting your love. I accept your love, I accept your pardon and grace, and I accept your words, "Go now and do likewise."

I believe, so I want to make you the pattern of my life.

You gave your life for others; I want to give my life for others.

You used your understanding to know your Father's will. I want to use my mind enlightened by faith to know his will for me.

You loved your Father and you loved me, and because you did, you won the battle in Gethsemane. You chose to give your life to save me from my sin. Lord, strengthen me, for I fear such love; I am afraid to take it as a pattern for my life. Yet I want to.

Mary, the angel told you to *fear not*. Teach me not to be afraid to love.

SCRIPTURE PASSAGE

"After this, Jesus, knowing that all was finished said in order to fulfill the scriptures, 'I thirst.'"

EXPLORE THE MEANING
AND MESSAGES OF THE PASSAGE

St. John describes his purpose in writing his Gospel in these terms: "There were many other signs that Jesus worked in the sight of the disciples, but they are not recorded in this book. These are recorded so that you may believe that Jesus is the Christ, the Son of God, and that believing this you may have life through his name."

In other words, he describes real events so that through them we will discover a reality that is not visible: that Christ is the Son of God. Once we know who Christ is, the eternal Son of God, we will be able to enter into the overwhelming mystery of how much God loves us, giving his life to save us.

So in John we have these two poles: he insists on the reality, physicality, and humanity of Christ on the one hand ("We speak to you of what we saw with our own eyes, touched with our hands…"), and the invisible mystery that those same, tangible, human realities hide and reveal at the same time (Jesus is the Christ, the Son of God).

1. First thirst: an extreme, physical thirst
Importance of the Physical for John

God's love was not something theoretical or abstract for John. It was real, concrete, overwhelming, and therefore undeniable. Some people in

John's day found it too much to say that God died for us on the cross, and some of them said he only appeared to be human, or he only appeared to die. Therefore, John goes out of his way to insist on the fact that Jesus was God and at the same time truly man, and his death was real.

The Reality of Christ's Crucifixion

The people John was speaking to, unlike us, were all too familiar with crucifixion. Many of them would have seen one firsthand and heard the delirious criminals cry out in their torture for something to drink, because the greatest suffering of crucifixion was thirst. John is trying to make sure his audience understands and accepts the enormity of what is happening. Jesus was really crucified, his suffering was real and not staged, his death was real and not imaginary. Therefore, his love is real.

Shake Off Routine

This cry of Jesus from the cross must help us break through our routine insensitivity at seeing Christ on the cross. The crucifix seems normal to us, yet it is the image of a man hanging from a cross by nails through his hands and feet, in agony with pain and thirst, his breath coming in gasps, nearing death. Crucifixion was so horrible a death that it was against Roman law to inflict in on a Roman citizen.

So, when John tells us Christ said, "I thirst," he wants us to break through any false illusions. Christ really died in agony, tortured for our sins. Let us not forget either the other sufferings he went through: the scourging, the crowning with thorns, the constant beatings, and the humiliations.

Learn and Accept the Cost of Love

Jesus suffered all this for me. He really and truly gave his life for me. This is the measure of his love. This also corrects our idea of love and gives us a new understanding of what love really is.

Jesus loved till it hurt, and beyond hurt. We have to learn this lesson, because love is fine for us as long as it doesn't hurt, but as soon as it means giving up something (a plan, a dream, or a possession, never mind my life), we begin to wonder if it is worth it.

Christian love, priestly love, costs us our life.

2. Second thirst: a spiritual thirst for souls
The Case of the Samaritan Woman

In John 4, we find a conversation about thirst that will help us discover a new level of meaning to Christ's "I thirst" on the cross. Let us read it and comment on it.

"On the way, they came to a Samaritan town called Sychar, near the land that Jacob gave to his son Joseph. Jacob's well was there and Jesus, tired because of the journey, sat straight down by the well. It was about the sixth hour. When a Samaritan woman came to draw water Jesus said to her, 'Give me a drink.' ("I'm thirsty" and "give me a drink" are two ways of saying the same thing). *And the woman said to him, 'What, you're a Jew, and you ask me, a Samaritan, for a drink?'* (John explains that Jews and Samaritans don't associate with each other). *And Jesus replied, "If you only knew what God is offering, and who it is that is saying to you: Give me a drink. You would have been the one to ask, and he would have given you living water."*

See where the conversation is going? He asks for a drink and she says, "How come you're asking me?" Jesus then turns things totally upside down, saying, "If you knew the gift of God, if you knew who I am, you would ask me for a drink instead." So now the woman is completely confused. She says, "You have no bucket. The well is deep. How will you give me this living water? Are you greater than our father Jacob who made this well?" Then Jesus pushes it farther: "If you drink from this water you will thirst again; if you drink from the water that I will give you, you will never be thirsty again. And the water I will give

91

will turn into a spring inside you, giving you eternal life." And then she goes on to ask for that water. So Jesus by saying he thirsts and asking for a drink on the Cross, is actually trying to offer us something.

The Banquet

What else could Jesus possibly be thirsting for? What does he want to give us? Christians have always understood that Christ is speaking about his thirst for souls.

Jesus says as much in a parable he told about a man who prepares a banquet. When he sent out the invitations people didn't want to come, and they made many excuses. He sent out servants to find other people to fill the hall in their place.

On the cross we have the banquet of his body and blood. He wants us to come and eat. He is thirsting and hungry to be able to feed us. He knows we need to eat his flesh and drink his blood if we are to have life in us. He doesn't want us to walk away from the source of life, for our own good.

Who Needs Whom?

On the cross, Christ is the Eucharist, our salvation. And he is saying, "Come to me. I am thirsting for you. Come to me all you that labor and are heavy burdened and I will give you rest." He is saying, "Here are the waters; here is the richness of life I want to give you. Come, I am thirsting for you because I have done this for you. I don't to send you away unfed lest you faint on the way. Come, partake of the fruits of my sacrifice. I want to see you renewed, with life in you." It is the thirst of his love for us that wants us to have what we need.

So Jesus, by saying, "I am thirsty," is calling us: "I want you to come and drink from this water. I am thirsting for your thirst, I am thirsting for you to come to feed here. I am thirsting for you to come to drink here." After

Christ has paid this price for our sins and redeemed us on the cross, what would be the worst insult we could give God, if not rejecting his salvation?

God's Joy; the Cross, the Source of Forgiveness

God helps us realize our own spiritual thirst and need. If we can imagine the hurt that snubbing him and his sacrifice would cause, we can also imagine his joy if we do accept his invitation, and go to him.

This joy is especially there when we go to him in the sacrament of reconciliation, confession. He is thirsting to give us the forgiveness he has earned for us, thirsting for us or us to come to have our life restored or strengthened.

At times we think that when we go to him with our weaknesses we will disappoint him. When we fail and something big goes wrong in our lives, the first way the devil tempts us is to say, "You could never go back to Christ like that, it's too big. God is not going to have time for you." If God has already paid the price for our sins, what Christ says to us from confession is, "I am thirsting for you. I want you to come. I want you to drink of this water. I want you to take this salvation to yourself. I don't want you to continue to be lost out there on your own."

And why is it, when we do come to confession, that once we do place our sins before God, there is an enormous flow of peace that comes into our soul? And with the sorrow for our sins, there is the joy of having been forgiven our sins.

We all, because of our pride, find it difficult to admit our failures. But sometimes we even have the idea that if we go to confession there is something that he won't want to forgive. But listen to him and ask, how would it be possible that God would not want to forgive our sins, if we place no obstacle to him?

Sometimes we are afraid of being rejected if we open ourselves up to him and humble ourselves before him. And sometimes the human instrument that he uses is to blame for that. But it is God who we go to confess our sins to, and Christ is thirsting for us to come.

Every time you go to confession, you can imagine Christ whispering, "It was worth it to die on the cross for this."

So, Christ is thirsting, he wants us to come. His open side is an invitation for us to come and take of all that he has done for us on the cross. I think we can keep on delving a little bit deeper on another level into this thirst of Christ that he is undergoing and which is expressed on the cross.

3. Third thirst: a thirst for coworkers, apostles
Always Working through Others

Remember when Christ multiplied the bread and gave it to the people? He didn't do all the work himself. He had his apostles look for bread and find the boy with the loaves and fish. After he said the blessing, he didn't give the bread to the people himself—"He gave the bread to his disciples and they gave it to the people." Jesus is always using instruments, those chosen people to reach and feed the rest.

It is a pattern that he follows to this day. He himself commands us to bring his words to all the nations. He doesn't say, "I will go to all nations," but "Go out to the whole world."

Power that Is Powerless on Its Own

This is by choice. On the cross and in the Eucharist, Christ shows his extreme power. But at the same time, the means he chose seem to handicap him and make it impossible for his power to reach out. He is nailed to the cross, and in the Eucharist he is "imprisoned" in the appearance of bread.

He cannot go anywhere; he does not speak audibly. People have to come to him, or he has to be brought to people. Even though he speaks to our souls, people have to be led to him spiritually, and we have to speak his message for it to be heard.

What has this got to do with the thirst of Christ on the cross?

Christ on the cross thirsts for workers and apostles, people who will be his coworkers in the work of redemption.

He thirsts for those who will come to him on the cross, receive everything from him, and then go and bring him to others and bring others to him... people who will share his thirst for souls.

His apostles are those who will bring him where he wants to go, but where he himself has decided he will not go unless he's brought.

He needs our lips to speak his message of salvation. He needs our feet to go to where the need is, to reach the farthest corners of the earth, to enter the world of business, politics, the arts, and education. He needs our hands to give out the food of salvation and to show his love and his mercy in our works. He needs our minds to be possessed by him, to understand and transmit him. He thirsts for them.

This another level of Christ's thirst on the cross. It is not a passive but an active thirst. He seeks apostles who will come to the cross, be transformed by his love and take his example of love as their model and program of life.

Why should this gift that God has given me be limited to me alone? I must go and bring him to others. We say to Christ on the cross and in the Eucharist, "Lord, where do you want me to go? If you're thirsting on the cross, where do you want to go? Where do you want me to bring you?"

An Apostolic Heart

He thirsts especially for those he has already chosen to dedicate their lives fully and exclusively to spreading his salvation. He thirsts that they will respond to the extraordinary love he has for them in calling them to this service.

So, when we spend this time in meditation at the feet of Christ on the cross, and when we hear him say those words, "I thirst," we can also hear him asking us, "Will you be the one that will spread these gifts others?" Christ is looking for those who will cooperate with him; he is thirsting for those who will help give the riches of his redemption to all those around us.

4. Fourth thirst: solidarity with the world that thirsts

Another aspect of Christ's thirst comes our in Matthew 25. You are familiar with Christ's description of the last judgment. The Son of Man will come, all the peoples of the earth will gather before him, he will separate them, putting some on his right and the rest on his left, and he will say to those on his right, "Come, you whom my father has blessed, and take for your heritage the kingddom prepared for you since the foundation of the world. For I was hungry and you gave me food. I was thirsty and you gave me drink. I was a stranger and you made me welcome. I was naked and you clothed me; sick and you visited me; in prison and you came to see me." They will answer, Lord, I'm confused, we lived in different centuries. "When did I ever see you naked and clothed you? When did I ever see you hungry and feed you? When did I ever see you thirsty and give you to drink?"

Listen to what Christ tells them, "The king will answer, 'I tell you solemnly, in so far as you did it to the least of these brothers of mine, you did it for me.'"

Christ Thirsting in the World

"I was thirsty."

So when Christ says to us from the cross, "I thirst," he speaks to our consciences in the name of all who thirst—those who suffer physical want and those who suffer spiritual want.

If he thirsts for souls, they also thirst for his redemption. Even those who have no physical wants, and sometimes they more than anyone else, thirst for the truth and thirst for redemption.

So he cries out from the cross in the name everyone who needs us in their poverty, be it physical or spiritual.

Let us look at the spiritual thirst of those around us. Those who seek happiness in so many ways and cannot find it, slipping into despair. Those who search for meaning in their lives and do not find it. Those who knew Christ and put him aside, and in their lives are paying with tears of bitterness, frustration, and humiliation because they see their lives slipping into something they don't want to be. He's speaking for those who never knew him, those who will know him someday only to have their joy tinged with disappointment, "You are a Christian, why did you wait so long to give me what I needed?"

Open Your Eyes and See Him

We sometimes think it would be easier to serve Christ if we saw him in the flesh. But we have him "in the flesh" in our neighbor. If those around me are thirsting, it is Christ who is thirsting.

There is a great thirst for God all around us. Maybe even in your own family, maybe your brothers and sisters, cousins, aunts, uncles, and parents.

The world is full of people seeking happiness, a meaning to life, and fulfillment. They are begging it from material things and possessions, friendships, success, and evading it in sex, alcohol, and drugs, all too often ending in despair. The world is full of those who suffer, who feel their life is wasted, who face failure.

Sinning by Omission

Not sharing the treasure of our faith, even the "hard sayings" of Christ that have to do with his moral expectations, is a terrible omission.

Our fear holds us back; so does our human respect.

Or it may be our laziness to delve into and understand the teachings of Christ so as to be able to articulate them well. People often don't recognize their own thirst until they begin to have it satisfied.

This is the thirst of our world today. It is a thirst for the faith that we have, for the meaning that Christ gives to our lives. It's a thirst for the happiness that comes from forgiveness, the hope that comes from God's presence with us.

Sinning by Pride, Superiority

And there is another truth, this one more chilling to us who think we are on the way of life. How do we look at the world around us? We often feel superior because we are *not like the rest of men*. We know our faith. We try to practice our faith. The "world" is a bad influence to be avoided. And so, instead of going out to give what we have, we turn inwards; we think only of ourselves. We retreat into a nice, comfortable group of friends, and become the "separated ones." Do you know what the name *Pharisee* means? That's it, the "separated ones." And they were the first ones to keep Christ and his apostles at bay.

I Thirst

Christ wants to remind us from the cross that those who have not heard his message, those who have heard it only partially, or those who have heard of him and have fallen away (a friend, the guy down the hall in my dorm...) are thirsting for what he has given us. We've got to give it to them. We can't go through life just feeling that we're so privileged, that God has been so good to us, and not hear the world calling out, "I thirst."

If we don't listen to their cry, and if we don't go out to give what we have, we are turning Christ himself down.

Christ in Others

We hear Christ call out from the cross saying, I thirst," and say, "If I were there I would've done something for you," as if his thirst were something of the past. It is now time to listen to Christ saying, "But I am right here. All you have to do is stretch out your hand and you'll find me in your college dorm, in your family, in your friends... and I'm thirsty, thirsty."

Listen to Christ on the cross saying, "I thirst." Listen to him saying, "If I thirst and you give me to drink, I will welcome you into heaven."And our indifference could spell death for that soul.

Someone will say to him on the last day, "Lord, why did you never give me your words of salvation?" and will he have to answer, "Well, actually I did send somebody, but there he was, locked in his room. I gave him skills to write and teach, and he never did; I gave him opportunities, grace, I came into his life, I showed him my love, but he kept it all for himself."

CONCLUSIONS

Spend some personal time with Christ. Talk this over with him. Let us break through the shell that builds up around our mind and spirit.

Christ's passion was real. His death was real. His thirst and suffering were real. These all show that his love for you and me was real. We need to spend time contemplating the actual sufferings Christ went through, asking him "Why, why, why?"

His desire to give us the fruits of his suffering is a real thirst. He thirsts to receive us in the sacrament of forgiveness.

His love is a missionary thirst, wanting to reach out, wanting to draw us into his action for souls. He is thirsting for apostles. When he says, "I thirst," he is inviting you to be his apostle. Have you heeded this invitation of Christ to be his messenger to others?

Not only is Christ thirsting to reach souls, but souls are thirsting for him. He does not want us to be deaf to that thirst. He identifies himself with every suffering and thirsting soul. Not to heed them, not to serve them, to keep the message for ourselves is to reject Christ.

COLLOQUIES

There is much to talk about with Christ.

Go slowly over the conclusions, and speak with him about each point.

Ask him if you are doing what you should. Examine the use you are making of his gifts (especially his sacraments) and ask him if you are heeding his call to be his apostle.

Ask him if your ears and heart are truly open to the needs of those around you, for not to serve them is not to serve him.

PART III

In this part of our retreat we are going to look at the experiences of four people in following Christ, not so much in order to examine their subjective feelings or experiences as to discover how Jesus approached and treated them, for he probably will deal with us in somewhat the same fashion. The conditions for following him will be the same, the promises he makes will be the same, and the difficulties they had to overcome will probably shed light on ours.

"Do You Love Me? Follow Me!"

JOHN 21:15-19

ENTERING INTO THE PRESENCE OF GOD

Lord Jesus, once more I am here before you. Once more I make the effort to open my soul, mind and heart to your words and example. I know you are present here in the Eucharist thanks to the gift of faith you gave me in baptism. I know you are here, and so I can speak to you and listen to you. I thank you for this gift, because without it I would not know what to do now.

I hope in you for the graces I need. I trust in you because I know that before I ask you for it, you already know what I need and want to give it to me. So if I do my prayer and try my best, following your lead, I know I will receive the graces I need to do things you are asking of me.

I want to love you, but not as I have been doing up to now. I want to start loving you as you deserve and as you taught me to love. I see your endless patience, your service, the way you treated Peter and the apostles and anyone who follows you. Endless love, seeking others to continue your love and be your coworkers. Thirsting for them.

Mary, you knew Peter well and you loved him too. You knew his struggles and surely you prayed for him. Teach me how to love.

SCRIPTURE PASSAGE

"When they had eaten, Jesus said to Simon Peter, 'Simon son of John, do you love me more than these others do?' He answered, 'Yes, Lord, you know I love you.' Jesus said to him, 'Feed my lambs.'

"A second time he said to him, 'Simon son of John, do you love me?' He replied, 'Yes, Lord, you know I love you.' Jesus said to him, 'Look after my sheep.'

"Then he said to him a third time, 'Simon son of John, do you love me?' Peter was hurt that he asked him a third time, 'Do you love me?' and said, 'Lord, you know everything; you know I love you.' Jesus said to him, 'Feed my sheep. In all truth I tell you, when you were young you put on your own belt and walked where you liked; but when you grow old you will stretch out your hands, and somebody else will put a belt round you and take you where you would rather not go.' In these words he indicated the kind of death by which Peter would give glory to God. After this he said, 'Follow me.'

EXPLORING THE MEANING
AND MESSAGES OF THE PASSAGE

1. The circumstances

After the resurrection Jesus sent his apostles up to Galilee to wait there for him. And while they waited they still had to eat, so Peter goes fishing and the others join him. They spend the whole night fishing and catch absolutely nothing.

Dawn comes and someone on the shore tells them where to let down their nets. They do so, and when the nets come up full to the tearing point John says, "It is the Lord." Peter jumps into the water to hurry to shore. They were only about a hundred yards from land, but Peter doesn't have the patience to wait as they row the overloaded boat in. And Jesus has breakfast prepared for them.

2. The triple question

When they had all eaten, Jesus drops what could have been a

bombshell. In front of everyone he asks Simon Peter, "Simon, son of John, do you love me more than these others do?" They all had heard Peter's boast at the Last Supper, that even though they all ran away, he would never betray Jesus. Now, in front of them Jesus asks Peter the question point-blank. It may have caused a stunned and embarrassed silence from some who couldn't believe Jesus had asked such a direct and potentially devastating question. It hung in the air. Peter had to answer.

Peter answers, "Yes, Lord, you know I love you." Jesus had asked, "… more than these?" What happened to Peter's presumption? "Even if everyone else walks out on you Lord, I won't. I will even die for you." Peter doesn't return there. He has a clearer idea of himself now. And Jesus says, "Feed my lambs."

It didn't end there. As the conversation returned to normalcy after Peter's answer, Jesus again asks, "Simon, do you love me?" He has dropped the comparison, "more than the others"; he is getting Peter to examine his own words. And Peter says, "Yes, Lord, you know I love you. And Jesus says, "Look after my sheep."

But, amazingly, Jesus does not let up. He presses a third time, "Simon, son of John, do you love me?" And now Peter reacts differently. "Peter was hurt that he asked him a third time…."

3. Peter's hurt

Why is Peter hurt? Does he realize he doesn't love Christ, or does he think Christ no longer trusts him?

Or does he really does love Christ, but now he remembers the last time something like this happened and Jesus insisted? It was at the Last Supper, and back then he was so full of presumption that he didn't heed what Christ was telling him. Perhaps he thought that maybe Christ was telling him now that his love was not as strong as he thought it was. Was Peter afraid he would betray his love again?

Peter's answer is beautiful; it is total abandonment. There is only one thing Peter knows, that Christ knows the truth about him.

"You know everything, you know I love you." He promises nothing of himself. He doesn't say, "I will never let you down," or "I will always do your work," or "I will never fail you." All he can do is make a statement: "Lord, you know I love you. Maybe my love is weak. Maybe my love can be very easily tossed and toppled. But I love you." Jesus said, "Feed my sheep."

4. The promise

And then Jesus says something more wonderful still to Peter. "When you were young you put on your own belt and walked where you liked; but when you grow old you will stretch out your hands, and somebody else will put a belt round you and take you where you would rather not go."

In other words, when you were young you did your own will, but that will change. A time will come when they will take you where you would rather not go. And John makes this explanation, "In these words he indicated the kind of death by which Peter would give glory to God."

To see just how wonderful a promise it is, remember how Jesus prayed in the Garden. "Father, if it is possible, take this chalice away from me, but not my will but yours be done." So we can say that when Jesus was led to his passion, he was going where he *would rather not go*.

Peter didn't want Jesus to go there either, for when Jesus first spoke of his passion and death he said, "Lord, this cannot be," and when the guards come to take Jesus prisoner Peter fights to defend him, cutting off the ear of one of them. He did not want to let Jesus go *where he would rather not go*, and when there was a danger of him being taken off as well, he fled.

But now Jesus is promising Peter that he will follow his Master up to death (what Peter had promised in the Last Supper but was not able to live up to a few hours later), that he would have the strength to be like him and be faithful, *going where he would prefer not to be led*. What a great promise!

So Jesus tells Peter, "Now that you truly love me, now that you don't depend on yourself, now that you put me at the center and recognize your own weakness, you will at last be what you always wanted to but never could be, because you depended on yourself and not on me, and there was love for yourself and pride mixed in with your love for me."

Peter now accepts Jesus on his terms, not his own. Before, Peter loved Jesus, but not above all things. He loved *his* idea of Jesus, the Jesus that was his kind of Messiah. He is naturally inclined to the limelight and being in the first place. Perhaps he relishes seeing the Pharisees squirm. He definitely looked to himself for his strength, but now he finds it in love.

Once Peter knows how weak he is, yet also knows he loves Jesus, this is when Jesus can bank on him, use him, give him the care of his sheep and lambs, and know that he will be faithful until death.

This is the watershed in Peter's life. Make it your watershed in this retreat.

5. Your conversation with Christ

Put yourself in Peter's place in front of Christ, and let him ask you the same questions.

First Question:

"Do you love me more than these others do?" That's how we'd like it to be—our vanity at work. And sometimes we actually do think we love God more than everyone else. We compare; we are judgmental against those who may have had less opportunities. And yes, we quickly excuse our own faults.

Let the implications of Jesus' question sink in. Answer honestly. *Do I still think I love Jesus more than others, that I'm the best thing that ever happened to Jesus? Do I still judge others and feel superior? Or have I changed, grown more like Christ?* Is your answer to Jesus still, "Yes, I do love you more than others," or have you learnt your lesson?

Or have you blocked out all comparisons as futile and as so many distractions to answer simply, "You know I love you."

Let us take a little liberty. When he asks us, "Do you love me more than the others do?" let us adapt it to "Do you love me more than you love everything else?" It's easy to admit we don't love him more than other people do, but it is harder to admit there are other things that we love more than him, things outside him that have caught our heart, or plans we nourish for ourselves that are not exactly his. We would give them up to a certain degree, but we quickly reach a threshold we are unwilling to cross.

Jesus said, "What does it profit a man to gain the whole world if he loses his soul?" but we exchange it for much less than the whole world: some vanity, pleasure, or people's opinion. Is there anything that, when I put it in the balance, wins out over Christ's love?

Second Question

Let him ask you a second time, this time dropping the comparison as he did for Peter. "Do you love me?"

In other words, let him ask you about the quality of your love. What does it make you do? Many of you are giving years of service to the Church. When Christ asks you, "Do you love me?" you can honestly answer that one thing your love for him has brought you to do is to give a year of your life exclusively to him to do his work. How many other actions in your life were or are motivated by your love for him?

The more you grow in your love, the more you do for him. You used to pray before; do you pray better now? Is your prayer changing your heart? You used to offer up sacrifices before; do you now? Take your pulse and see if your love for Christ is getting you to do things, because that is the sign of true love. Love is not limited to the way I react when faced with a choice, love is proactive, moving me actively to choose to do certain things and to behave in a certain way. If I love, I won't merely choose to be faithful to Christ when I am faced with temptation, I will set out to do as much as I can for him.

So the second question makes us reflect on the type of love we have for him.

Third Question

Let Jesus insist a third time, "Do you love me?"

The third question hurt Peter, because he realized his own weakness. He realized how easily he let Jesus down, ran away to the point of cursing and swearing that he did not know him.... It all comes flooding back. As Paul said later, "We carry this treasure in vessels of clay." Because of who we are, our Christian life is necessarily fragile, there's no getting away from it. And as with St. Peter and this third question, remember your weakness.

We have often let Jesus down. When he asks us to love him, or asks something special of us, we should never forget this. To love him like we ought, we need his help. We need his grace. We need to be humbly at the feet of Jesus to ask his help, and not looking for the source of our fidelity in ourselves.

Jesus knows how weak we are, but it seems he cannot trust us with his work until we know and recognize it ourselves. It was only when Peter felt the hurt that Jesus was finally able to promise him he would be his martyr. Only when the call surprises us, and it confuses us that God should choose us, being so weak, are we ready to begin to follow it.

So let Jesus ask his question a third time, and each one of us in our own heart is going to admit his weakness. If we have any serious unconfessed sins, this admission has to be made within the sacrament of confession for it to be fruitful. If there are not, a devotional, general confession will still be very helpful in order to savor God's mercy once more and grow in humility.

How unworthy we are of Christ's love! How we need his grace to transform us in order to love him as we ought, to persevere in our love for him, to let him do with our lives and ask of us things we would sooner walk away from! If we could only love as sincerely and humbly as Peter, perhaps he could make that great promise to us as well, guaranteeing us that we will be like him and follow in his footsteps: "Someday somebody will lead you where you do not want to go. You are going to become just like me, despite your weakness. You are going to give glory to God in the way you live, in the way you follow me, in what you do, and in the way you spend your life for me."

This is the paradox, the contradiction when we come close to God and try to do his work. It has got to be him that works in us. If we're trying to figure out what God wants us to do in our lives, we shouldn't be looking at how strong and great and perfect we think we are; we should be looking at how strong and how great Jesus is. And if we love him enough and let him into our lives to heal the weakness there is in us, he can make us his instruments to do his work.

CONCLUSIONS

So, let Jesus ask you three times, "Do you love me?"

Are you focused on him without comparing yourself to others? Do you love him above all other things and people?

How deep is your love? Are you seeking to do as much as you can for him, or is you love still very much defined by materially keeping the commandments and no more?

Is my love based on my humble knowledge of myself, and absolute trust in him, to let him lead me with joy wherever he wants, even where I would rather not go?

Notice how different Christ's approach is to our own. Before saying "Follow me," he asks, "Do you love me?"

Yet when wondering if we will follow him, we don't usually start by asking "Do I love you?" Our question is usually, "Have I got all of this figured out? Are all the guarantees in place? Am I sure I can do it? Is it really to my liking?"

It is time to make adjustments.

Spend some time with our Lord here as he looks at Peter. It is a wonderful moment when we see this contrast of humility, goodness—all the goodness and sincerity that Jesus always saw in him but nobody else did. Speak to the patient and gentle Jesus even though the questions shock us at first. We see Jesus' grace and patience paying off here in Peter's life.

Lord, love and not pride was what made Peter the Rock of your Church. Love and not pride was the way you came to save us, doing your Father's will. You did not hold onto your honors, but you humbled yourself and became my servant.

If I were to ask you, "Do you love me?" you have already given your answer in your life. I was your lost sheep and you found me and fed me.

I want to love you, and to help you find and feed your sheep. You will be my strength, and you will be my guide.

Christ Takes Over Paul's Life
ACTS 7:59; 8:1-3; 9:1-25

ENTERING INTO THE PRESENCE OF GOD

Lord Jesus, once more I am here in your presence, for a meditation in which I am sure all the graces that have been accumulating over the day will begin to bear very specific fruit in my soul.

My heart is as open, or more open, than when I started on this retreat. How can I close it when I see your example? I have rediscovered so much about you and your love for me, so much about myself and the gift of life, and the price that you paid for my sins. And I hear you calling for followers, thirsting for apostles to continue your work. I have seen that your love is real, not something abstract but something real that I have seen and has touched me—in the gift of life, in my redemption, in your forgiveness.

It is with a heart filled with renewed faith that I begin this meditation. I am full of confidence and trust. You know what I need even before I ask for it. You know what I need to be the person you expect me to be, to do the work that you want me to do, to be the consolation that you have always wanted me to be. So, I come here to receive those graces that I already hope and know that I will receive.

And I want to continue to grow in my love for you, to discover the love that moves everything you do so that love will become the reason for all my actions too. If anything I want to do does not stem from love, let me set it aside so as to do something more worthwhile that will be more full of love for you and for others. I cannot truly follow you without loving you. I am poor and weak, so I come to you, the fountain of all goodness and life. I come to you because I am poor and needy.

Mary, lead me in my thoughts and my reflections. Help me to say *"Be it done unto me"* when God makes his will known, and to become a servant of the Lord.

EXPLORE THE MEANING
AND MESSAGES OF THE PASSAGES
1. Introduction

The story of St Paul's conversion has much to tell us, and so we are going to walk through it, trying to appreciate the power of God's grace and the need to respond to it with all our hearts.

We find it in the Acts of the Apostles at the end of chapter 7, the beginning of chapter 8, and then in chapter 9.

2. The story

We see Paul for the first time at the stoning of Stephen, where immediately he takes off in the wrong direction—from a bystander into a persecutor of the Church. Apparently, Stephen was to blame.

Stephen had been called before the Sanhedrin and ordered not to preach about Jesus, because to them it was blasphemy. He is unrepentant and right there in their presence the Book of Acts tells us he is filled with the Holy Spirit, gazes into heaven, and cries out, *"'Look, I can see Heaven thrown open and the Son of Man standing at the right hand of God.' And all the members of the council shouted out and stopped their ears with their hands and made a concerted rush on him and thrust him out of the city and they stoned him.* [And here Saul (Paul's old name) surfaces]*...and the witnesses put their clothes down at the feet of a young man called Saul. And as they were stoning him, Stephen said in invocation, 'Lord, receive my Spirit!' And then he knelt down and said aloud, 'Lord, do not hold this sin against them.' Then Stephen died."*

3. Saul's development

Apparently, things happened quickly with Paul. Look at the progression: "...the witnesses put down their clothes at the feet of a young man called Saul." So, he does not take part in the stoning;something seems be holding him back, something that snaps right there and then as he looks on, because the change is immediate. We read that Saul approved of the killing.

The reason for the change must be in the words and actions of Stephen. "Lord Jesus, receive my Spirit, and, Lord, do not hold this sin against them."

Not only does he call Jesus his Lord, he also treats Jesus as if he were God—because he says to Jesus, "Receive my Spirit," and God is the one who receives the spirit after death. He says, "Do not hold this sin against them," and only God can forgive sins. On top of it all, he speaks to this dead Jesus as someone living!

Now, Saul knows that Jesus was dead. And Stephen is speaking to him and treating him like God. To Saul's ears this is blasphemy, and it calls for action.

4. Saul's convictions

In Saul's mind Stephen is not simply mistaken, he is terribly wrong; his words are offensive, a blasphemy against the One, Living God. So Saul's mind is made up. Men who believe and say such things must die.

Saul is now committed, and when he reappears in Acts the book has this to say: "*Saul then began doing great harm to the Church and he went from house to house arresting both men and women, and sending them into prison.*"

He has rapidly progressed from undecided to decided and then to committed. It's clear to him that if all Christians believe the same as Stephen, they all deserve to die. This is no time for lame wrist-slapping. This is blasphemy, and Saul will see to it that Christians either change or die.

The pace accelerates. Saul's zeal is ferocious, and he branches out from Jerusalem. We read, "*Meanwhile, Saul was still breathing threats to slaughter the Lord's disciples. He went to the high priests and asked for letters addressed to the synagogues in Damascus that would authorize them to arrest and take to Jerusalem any followers of the way, men or women that he might find.*"

Look at his threats—not to imprison but to slaughter the Lord's disciples, every single one he can lay his hands on. So, his purpose in going to Damascus "to arrest and take to Jerusalem any followers of the way, men or women that he might find," was to slaughter them.

Saul was first of all on the fringes, unable to make up his mind. Then he realized that Stephen believed that Jesus was still alive and was God. But that cannot be, it is blasphemy, Stephen had to die. He quickly understands that all Christians believe the same about Jesus, and he concludes that Christians must change or die. He did it in Jerusalem and he is on his way to do as much in Damascus.

Damascus

We must understand the depth and strength of these convictions of Saul in order to appreciate the impact of what comes next.

"It happened that while he was traveling to Damascus and approaching the city, suddenly a light from Heaven shone all around him. And he fell to the ground and then he heard a voice saying, 'Saul, Saul, why do you persecute me?' 'Who are you, Lord?' he asked, and the answer came, 'I am Jesus whom you are persecuting. Get up and go into the city and you'll be told what to do.'"

Remember Saul's convictions: Jesus is dead, not alive. Jesus is not God, he is not Lord, he is not Master.

5. The revelation

Let us relive the scene more slowly.

The first words that he hears when he is knocked to the ground are, "Saul, Saul why are you persecuting me?" Who speaks from heaven? Saul tells us in his answer, because he addresses that voice by saying, "Who are you, Lord?" From the time he first learned to pray the Psalms, Saul had learned to call God Lord. And who else speaks from heaven?

Who are you, Lord? Put yourself in Saul's frame of mind. You are fully convinced that this Jesus is a hoax, that Christians are blasphemers, and for calling Jesus Lord they deserve to die. Then you hear these words from heaven, from the one you have called Lord, "I am Jesus"!

Jesus is not dead! I just called him Lord! Am I a blasphemer too?

"I am Jesus, whom you are persecuting." I am Jesus, I am alive, I am the Lord, I am God, and you have raised your hand against me.

Saul's life is now turned upside down. Everything he believes in comes crashing down. "It is not the Christians that are blasphemers. It's *you*, for saying I am not God. And you have raised your hand against me."

At that moment, without giving Saul a second to answer, Jesus simply moves in and takes over his life. "Get up and go into the city and there you'll be told what to do." Jesus simply begins to act like who he is, God and Master. He doesn't ask Saul's permission. He gives him no time to adjust. It seems like he says simply, "Now that you know who I am and how wrong you were, a new life is beginning. Let's get to work. Go into the city and somebody will tell you what you have to do."

Jesus knew the rugged, passionate Saul and treated him accordingly. In our own lives he tends to be softer, for he knows us too. Nevertheless, there are moments in which he seems to say to us as well, "Get up, stop wallowing, you have seen the light. Get up, make the change. Go forward and you will be told what to do." For he is the Lord, he is God, he is the one who made us, the one who redeemed us. He has all of these rights over us—rights that he exercises in love.

So he sends Saul into the city.

6. The test and the wait

This is a dramatic moment for Saul. "*The men traveling with Saul stood there speechless. For though they heard the voice, they could see no one. Saul got up from the ground and opened his eyes, whereupon he could see nothing at all. And they had to lead him into Damascus by the hand. For three days he was without his sight and he took neither food nor drink.*"

Saul has lost everything, including his sight and his dignity. This avenger of God who was swooping down at the head of his band to wreak havoc on the Church in Damascus is now helpless and lost.

Like a child, he has to be led by the hand. Who is going to tremble in terror of him now?

"He was three days fasting, taking neither food nor drink." To us it may sound like he's sulking, perhaps because that's how we react when God moves in and let's us know something we'd rather not. Resentment and sulking. That's us.

Saul was not sulking. Saul was preparing to meet God again. When the prophets went out to meet God, they would fast and pray in preparation. Paul is preparing with fasting and prayer because Jesus told him, "You will be told what you're to do." He is expecting God to come back and say his word to him.

Saul has changed. He knows Jesus is God. And when God tells you he is going to speak, you prepare with prayer and fasting to receive his word and do it.

7. The heroic messenger

At this point the Book of Acts cuts to another scene and introduces us to someone else in Damascus that Jesus puts on the spot.

"There was a disciple in Damascus called Ananias, and he had a vision in which the Lord said to him, 'Ananias!' And when he said, 'Here I am!' the Lord said, 'Get up and go Straight Street and ask at the house of Judas for someone named Saul, he comes from Tarsus. At this moment he is praying and he has seen a man named Ananias coming in and laying his hands on him to give him back his sight.'"

You have to love Ananias' answer. He says, *"Lord, I have heard from many people about this man and all the harm he has been doing to your holy people in Jerusalem. He has come here with a warrant from the chief priests to arrest anyone who invokes your name."*

Ananias is obviously saying, "Thanks, but no thanks" to God. In the most discreet way possible he tells him, "I'm not sure you have really thought this one through. Let me remind you what we're dealing with here. This man is dangerous. He did so much harm in Jerusalem and now has come here to do the same." Ananias is also hinting, "Lord, you know what will happen to me as your follower if I show up at his house." He was going through his own little Gethsemane. "Isn't there a better way to do whatever you have in mind?"

Does Jesus answer, "Ananias, don't you worry, everything will be OK"? No, he simply says, *"Go!"* No doubt here who is in charge, and he adds, *"This man is my chosen instrument to bring my name before Gentiles and kings for the people of Israel I myself will show him how much he must suffer for my name."* But there are no assurances for Ananias.

So Much in the Balance

The next few moments were pivotal for God's plan for his Church. History depended on the outcome of Ananias' internal struggle. In the balance is Saul receiving baptism. At stake is all he will go on to do for Christ, his life-long missionary outreach to the Gentiles.

Ananias could have walked away, and everything would have been different. It all hinged on his heroic obedience to Christ's command that really didn't seem to make much sense and was dangerous in the extreme.

So Ananias puts on his cloak, ties on his sandals, and walks out the door, not knowing if this is the last day of his life, if he is about to meet death at the hands of the soldiers with Saul, or if it will be prison and stoning at a later date.... Did he say good-bye to his family and friends?

But Jesus said "Go!" and Ananias went.

Friends, such is the Christian stock we are born from. We owe the faith we have today to so many anonymous Ananiases down through the centuries who put it all on the line to bring Christ's message to others, even to their enemies in the face of certain persecution and death.

Such is the blood that courses in our veins if we call ourselves Christians. Will we be worthy of our heritage and listen to Christ who sends us, or will we give into the fear that gnaws at our heart?

"Ananias went and entered the house; he laid his hands on Saul and said, 'Brother Saul, I have been sent by the Lord Jesus who appeared to you on your way here, so that you might recover your sight and be filled with the Holy Spirit.'"

Ananias has entered into God's way of doing things. He enters and lays his hands on Saul so that he could recover his sight and be filled with the Holy Spirit. On a human level, he makes Saul even more dangerous, because with Saul blind, Ananias at least has a chance to get away. Ananias put his hands on Saul so he can receive his sight and be filled with the Holy Spirit.

"It was as though scales fell away from his eyes and immediately he was able to see again. So he got up and was baptized and after taking some food he regained his strength." Saul gets up and is baptized. There is no hesitation on his part.

8. Saul's first up-close experience of Christians

"Brother Saul!"

Marvelous words for Ananias to utter. He is speaking to the persecutor of the Church. He most probably knew personally many of those who had died at Saul's hands, yet his first words to Saul are, "Brother Saul." On his walk to Straight Street as he reflected on Jesus' words and command, he had moved from his initial reluctance to fully accepting that Jesus intended to make Saul his messenger, and he had so understood Jesus' example that he had already embraced Saul in his heart as his brother. But he probably still didn't know if the price would be his own blood or not.

For Saul, this was his first living contact with what he would come to understand as the essence of Christ's message: charity. Paul is helpless, a Christian walks in... The Law said, "an eye for an eye, a tooth for a tooth," but instead, the first words he hears are "Brother

Saul," and the first action done to him by a Christian is "to give you the Holy Spirit... to give you your sight back." No rancor, no vengeance; only love, gifts. This Christian gives Saul all he has, just like the love of God who gives his life for the sinner.

9. Saul's new life

And to complete this picture of Saul, let us read on a few more verses, and then we will go back and draw a final lesson.

"After he had spent only a few days with the disciples in Damascus, he began preaching in the synagogues." And listen to what he was preaching—Jesus is the Son of God—which before was the exact reason he thought Stephen should be stoned. He preaches the self-same message he once persecuted.

Of course, *"all who heard were amazed and they said, 'Surely this is the man who did so much damage in Jerusalem to the people who invoked his name and who came here for the sole purpose of arresting them and to have them tried by the chief priests.'"*

Saul's power increased steadily and he caused great confusion among the Jewish colony at Damascus by the way he demonstrated that Jesus was the Christ.

And how does this passage end? *"Some time passed and the Jews worked out a plot to kill him."* Saul had been killing Christians. He became Christian, and now they were trying to kill him.

News of this got out. *"They were watching the gates at night to kill him. But the disciples took him by night and let him down from the wall, lowering him in a basket."* They put him in a basket, with ropes to let him down over the wall, courting death to avoid death. And so the new life of Saul began.

Such was the price of being a Christian, and no one better than Saul knew it. He knew when he was baptized that what he had done to Christians would be done to him.

10. Important lesson

What was the difference between Saul when he could not accept that Jesus was the Christ, and Saul when he was able to prove that Jesus was the Christ? Nobody could explain the change. Had he taken a crash course in theology? No. He spent those days in prayer and penance. He received baptism, and with it the gift of faith and the gifts of the Holy Spirit.

So, through the seemingly harsh means that God used of throwing him to the ground, humiliating him, and leaving him without his sight, he had been given a new sight. "Scales fell from his eyes," and from the eyes of his soul. The considerable knowledge he had of the Scriptures before his conversion never led him to accept Christ as the fulfillment of the law and the prophets. However, once he has been given the gift of faith, once he removes the obstacles to the work of God in his soul, that same knowledge bears fruit and becomes a means to help him demonstrate that Jesus is the Son of God.

Sometimes we think that to follow Christ sincerely and totally we need to know more things. No, we need only to know him, to increase our faith. Saul didn't know more things, but he discovered the living Christ, and life would never be the same.

CONCLUSIONS

What does this wonderful passage of Paul's conversion have to do with me? Why are we meditating on it at this stage of our retreat?

We have come to these exercises so that God can do to us what he did to Saul. Not to give us many more reasons, but to touch us in the way that each one needs. Some might still need to tumble from their horse. We all need to know and accept Jesus, but only he knows how each one needs to be touched.

And the purpose is to be set on fire, so that after this retreat we will not be afraid of ridicule, persecution, difficulties, or sacrifice.... So that we will give up our comfortable Christianity that would be unrecognizable to Saul and Ananias.... So that we will stop looking for more signs and simply use the gifts of faith, hope, and love we have already received, taking away any obstacle to the work of the Holy Spirit in our lives.

In Saul, we can see the power of God's grace. If he can change Saul, he can certainly change us.

COLLOQUIES

Take some moments on your own with Christ. Talk to him. Re-read the passages we have used; marvel at what Christ did with Saul. Marvel at how Saul responded. Admire Ananias the hero. Wonder at the power of Christian love.

And here before the Blessed Eucharist speak to the Lord and ask him a few questions.

"Lord, I believe that you are here present. Are you the same Jesus that appeared to Saul?" You know the answer.

"And at my baptism did I receive the same Holy Spirit as Saul?" The answer is obvious.

"Are your followers still called to the same courage in spreading your word and preaching your name, or has something changed?" There can only be one answer.

Then make a petition. "Lord, increase my faith so I can touch you as Saul did. You told Ananias that you were going to teach him how much he would have to suffer for you, and Saul never turned back. Help me when things get difficult and I feel like pulling back."

Think of the many people who have risked their lives throughout the centuries, martyrs that were faithful to the Faith so it might be passed onto you. See the many hidden Ananiases there, all through history—as close as the generation before you, maybe friends of yours—and see how God has been continually reaching out to you.

Say, "Lord, I want to do what Saul did. You told him to enter the city—that he would be told what he had to do and he prepared for it in fasting and in prayer. And when your word arrived he accepted it."

So this is an occasion for us to renew our faith in Christ who is risen and in the power and action of Christ in our life. He is not just an idea from our past. Christ is our life. Christ is our hope. Christ is our companion. Christ is looking for us, searching for us.

Let God's grace soak into your life. Examine your spirit to see what he is beginning to ask of you.

◈ ◈ ◈

Christ's Faithful and Invisible Presence

LUKE 24:13-35

Christ has not changed. It is the same Christ, the same Holy Spirit, and the same Church as it was in the time of St. Paul, so we should be aware and open to the change that Christ can operate in our souls. But we might have a question. We might have a doubt. It might seem to us that this looks fantastic when it happened to St. Paul, but in what way does Christ come to meet me in my life? I certainly have had no Damascus experience.

Maybe you can say to yourself, rightly, "I have not persecuted anyone like Saul persecuted the church. In what way is Christ going to come out and meet me?" And for that reason we're taking another passage of the Gospel to meditate on in this short meditation. We will read about something that happened after the Resurrection, later on that very same day.

ENTERING INTO THE PRESENCE OF GOD

Lord Jesus, in your presence I begin this last stage of my retreat. Some moments ago I received you in Communion. You are spiritually present within my soul with all the power of your divinity and all your grace and all the love that you have shown us always. I embrace you and thank you for the gift of your presence.

You are really present here before me in the Sacrament of the altar. The appearance of bread hides you from my eyes, but with the eyes of faith I know it is you, because it was in your power that the words were said, "This is my body" and "This is my blood." In your desire to "be with us always," you gave your power to your Church to make you present.

I believe in you, I believe in this sacrament, I believe in your Church.

I hope in you that in these final hours of my retreat I will extract all the good that you have prepared for me today, and bring to fruition all the reflections and graces you placed in my soul in each meditation up to now.

I hope that I will grow to love you as I sought, putting you before everything else and trying to love you in the same measure as you have loved me.

I thank **you** for your time with me. I thank you for the fidelity of so many generations of Christians that have handed down the faith to me, your sacraments, and your gifts. I thank you for the apostles that in every age have heeded your thirst, loved you, and followed you; those who did not fear persecution, who trusted in you in times of darkness. But for them, I would not be before you today.

Lord, call me, use me, send me so that your message will not end here, and your gifts will reach as many of my brothers and sisters as possible.

Mary, as the apostles I wish to be with one heart, joined constantly in prayer, with you the Mother of Jesus.

"Two of them were on their way to a village called Emmaus, seven miles from Jerusalem. And they were talking together about all that had happened, and it happened that as they were talking together and discussing it, Jesus himself came up and walked by their side. But their eyes were prevented from recognizing him. And he said to them, 'What are all these things that you are discussing as you walk along?' They stopped and their faces were downcast. And one of them called Cleophas answered him, 'You must be the only person staying in Jerusalem who does not know the things that have been happening there these past few days.' He asked, 'What things?' They answered, 'All about Jesus of Nazareth, he showed himself to be a prophet, powerful in action and speech before God and the whole people. And how our chief priests and our leaders handed him over to be sentenced to death and had him crucified. Our own hope had been that he would be the one to set Israel free. And this is not all. Two whole days have now gone by since all of this happened and some women from our group have astounded us. They went to the tomb in the early morning and when they could not find the body they came back to tell us that they had seen a vision of angels who declared that he was alive. Some of our friends went to the tomb and found everything exactly as the women had reported. But as for him, they saw nothing.'

And then he said to them, 'You foolish men, so slow to believe in all that the prophets have said. Was it not necessary that the Christ should suffer before entering into his glory?' And then he started with Moses and went through all the prophets and explained to them the passages throughout scripture that were about himself. When they drew near to the village to which they were going, he made as if he was going to go on, but they pressed him to stay with them, saying, 'It is nearly evening, and the day is almost over.' So he went in to stay with them. Now, when he was with them at table he took the bread and gave the blessing and then he broke it and handed it to them. And their eyes were opened and they recognized him. But he vanished from their sight. Then they said to each other, 'Did not our hearts burn within us as he talked to us on the road and explained the scripture to us?'"

EXPLORE THE MEANING
AND MESSAGES OF THE PASSAGE

We will take this passage slowly, because it applies so well to what we live each and every day.

1. Who were these two young men?

These two young men were heading back home from Jerusalem after their time with Jesus—two young men who at some stage had left everything to follow him. They left their homes and families for they hoped that "he would set Israel free." Perhaps they had been one of the chosen thirty-six teams of two, the seventy-two disciples Jesus sent out to preach in his name, and had actually received power over demons. These are two young men who had at some moment had said yes to Christ, opening their lives to him; however, their knowledge of Christ still hadn't grown or deepened. His full message hadn't gotten through to them.

They followed him, they heard his powerful preaching, they saw his miracles, they listened on the edge of their seats as he debated the Pharisees, and they too probably said in awe, "Nobody ever spoke like this man..., he preaches with authority, not like the Scribes."

2. Their problem

Nevertheless, their experience of Christ was superficial. They were close to him physically, but there remained a dimension they didn't understand, or hadn't entered into or accepted. Some weeks earlier, if you had asked them if they understood and were convinced of Christ, there would have been no doubt in their minds. "Yes, for sure. He is a prophet. He is the one who will set Israel free. We can trust him. He multiplied the bread. He heals. He drives out demons. Of course, we are convinced he's the Christ. He is the one to follow."

But here they are, on their way home to Emmaus, dejected, their faces downcast. Overnight, their faith in Christ had crumbled. "Yes, our own hope had been that he would be the one to set Israel free."

Their problem? Christ was gone; they could no longer see, touch, or listen to him. Christ could not be alive. They dismissed anything to the contrary as a made-up story, as we can see from their skeptical words, "When (the women) could not find the body they came back to tell us they had seen a vision of angels who declared that he was alive." Their own lack of faith made them unable to accept the words of those who did believe.

It happens to us, too. When Christ seems present and we can almost touch and feel him doing great things in our life we are quick to believe he is our Savior, we are enthusiastic beyond measure, he can ask anything of us and we'll do it. But let him hide a little, let the feelings subside, or let me be faced with a choice between something I really like and him—in other words, let the Cross and the reality of having to die to myself appear on the horizon…. Don't we walk away, our faces downcast? We thought it was going to be different, despite what Christ always told us. We are sorry it didn't work out. And we leave Jerusalem.

So, we really need to see how Christ dealt with these two young men and the problem we share with them.

3. Christ goes out to meet them and remains hidden at the same time

The first thing to notice is, though they are walking away from Jesus, he doesn't walk away from them, leaving them to their despair as if to say, "You had your chance." Christ today is the same Christ that went out to meet these two young men, although he did so in way they did not expect or recognize.

Most of our life is a struggle. We find it difficult to accept the cross that following him entails; we expect this to be cost-free. We react to the purification he lets us go through in times of darkness in our personal and spiritual life. But Christ always comes out to meet us. He simply is incapable of leaving us alone in our despair, shattered hopes, and sadness.

He comes and walks by our side. He has always been with us. He keeps seeking us out; he keeps working with us. However, most of the time we hardly recognize him. We think it is some stranger, a mere coincidence. It can be a word, an opportunity, a meeting, something I read, but when they are for our good it is always God there working through them.

So the Christ we are meeting on this retreat, the Christ that will walk with us after the retreat, won't walk out on us. When we are disheartened or discouraged and find the going difficult, when we are tempted to dump our resolutions and walk away, precisely then is when Jesus makes sure to be at our side.

4. Christ builds their faith by teaching them

The second thing to note is that Jesus doesn't do the obvious. Their problem was that they couldn't accept that he was alive, and so we would expect him to let them see him instead of hiding himself from them.

Why did he do differently? For Jesus, it was much more important that they believe in him rather than see him. They had already been with him for three years, yet they hadn't understood. Building their faith was more important than satisfying their senses and emotions, and Jesus foregoes the quick fix of pandering to their senses so as to awaken a greater gift, their faith.

During their time following Jesus, their faith was based on the miracles, their emotions, and their senses. It did not accept the cross, and it could not last. They couldn't imagine a presence of Christ that was not physical. And Jesus knew that "even if someone comes back to them from the dead they will not believe." Consequently, he wanted to go deeper, to build the house of their faith on rock, not sand. "They have Moses and the Prophets."

So he hides himself instead of revealing himself in a flash. Instead of an emotional reunion, he walks with them for hours and he painstakingly builds up their faith by teaching them. He began "with Moses and the Prophets, and he explained to them the passages throughout scripture that were about himself."

5. Christ rekindles the love that is not quite dead

Although they are walking away from Jerusalem because Jesus is dead and their dreams have been dashed, for some reason they can't seem to be able to get him out of their minds. As soon as they're asked what they were talking about, they are unable simply to say, "Oh, about Jesus who died." They have to tell the whole story, and there is something breathless about the way the words come tumbling out, "Jesus of Nazareth… showed himself to be a prophet, powerful in speech and in action, before God and the whole people (they are justifying why they had followed him)… handed over to death and crucified…We had hoped… that is not all, two whole days… some women of our group…."

6. Christ is firm

It would be great if there were some way to hear the tone of his voice as he said to them, "You foolish men!" It must have jolted them, but it did not offend them, and Jesus continues, "You are so slow to believe all the Prophets said."

If our Jesus bends to our every whim and never brings us up short, we have the wrong Jesus and not the Jesus of the Gospel.

The Jesus of the Gospel, our Savior, is always "the Way, the Truth and the Life." Since we are human, limited, and easily mistaken, he often has to tell us either directly in our hearts or through his representatives that we are being foolish.

The Christ we meet in Communion, the Christ we meet in the Gospels, the Christ that reaches out to us in the teachings of the Church on the moral life is the Christ who is not afraid to tell us the truth.

What happens to these men as they listen to Christ without knowing it is really him? What happens as they follow him and take in his every word?

7. Christ gives joy and purpose

Just like the rich young man who walked away sad from Jesus, these two men were utterly dejected as they wended their way home to Emmaus. But later on, to describe what happened to them as they listened to him and opened their hearts to the teaching and the faith that he was rekindling in them, they said, "Did not our hearts burn within us when he talked with us on the road and explained the Scripture to us?"

8. Mature faith

"Did not our hearts burn within us?" So much so, that when Jesus made to pass on and leave them, they wouldn't let him. They still didn't know it was him. When it is Jesus who speaks to us, even if his words are sometimes difficult, our hearts burn within us.

We live in a skeptical age where idealism is a bad word. When you get enthusiastic about something, people can't accept or understand because they don't have faith; you are suspect.

How difficult it is for our age to understand the heart that burns within us when we open it up to Christ and listen to him speak! How difficult it is for the rationalist to understand the truth and fire of love!

After walking with them, teaching them, showing them the way, and lighting this fire in their hearts, he sat down at table. He breaks the bread, blesses it, hands it to them, and… finally, they recognize him. But "in that same instant, as soon they recognize him, he disappeared from their sight." Being with Jesus, seeing him face-to-face, without any Sacrament between us, has to wait for heaven.

There is a great lesson in the young men's reaction. Instead of being frustrated, thinking Jesus was playing with them and their emotions, they have grasped the essence of the Resurrection. You don't have to see him, yet he is always there, he is risen, he is true to his word that he will always be with us.

Instead of being overcome with new sadness at the second disappearance of Jesus, they are filled with joy and new energy. They jump up and can't wait to get back to tell the others the great truth. "They hurried back to Jerusalem." You cannot keep Christ to yourself; you have to give him to others.

A mature faith is not based on the senses or on the emotions.

CONCLUSIONS

Christ is present. We don't have to see him. We don't have to feel his presence. Most of the time we don't, but he is still with us. The more we listen to his teaching, the more we understand him, and the more our hearts will be set on fire.

This is no superficial enthusiasm—it is faith. It is opening both our mind and our heart to God.

Christ is present in different ways in his Word, in his Church, in our neighbor, in his sacraments, in the Eucharist, and in his teachings. As long as they are with us, he is with us. When you think he has left you, or when you feel disheartened, recognize the Jesus who walks beside you and teaches you in his Church, the Jesus you can serve in your neighbor, and the Jesus who really and truly comes into your heart and soul, although in a way that is hidden from your senses in Communion. We are never alone.

COLLOQUIES

To end, simply thank Christ for the great gift of his presence.

Ask him forgiveness for the times of discouragement when you have walked away, even after knowing and experiencing him.

Resolve to live in faith and not on your feelings. Ask him for the grace to be as faithful a friend to him as he is to you.

CONCLUSION

This is our last meditation. In the time that is left it is important to be focused on what you are going to bring out of the retreat. I don't think any one of you began your retreat with the intention of being exactly the same when you ended as when you started. You knew you needed to change something, you knew you needed to do something, although you may not have been sure of what it was.

So now, with the lights you have received in the retreat focus what it is concretely that you need to change and need to do. You will probably have concrete things you know you need to do in your prayer from now on, your behavior, the direction you will give your life and the choices you need to make to get there.

In this final meditation we will go over the concrete pointers Christ himself gives us as regards keeping your resolutions and bearing fruit. In the process we will see once again how deeply he knows us and the obstacles we face. This in turn should renew our trust in him and our confidence in his help.

Bearing Fruit:
Christ's Practical Advice

LK 8:4-15

ENTERING INTO THE PRESENCE OF GOD

I begin this final meditation of my retreat in your presence with this petition: let all the seeds you have sown in my heart bear fruit. Help me to accept that you want me to bear fruit. You want my actions to reflect that I have met you and received your grace and to show you walk with me.

I believe in your presence in the Eucharist. Through your grace you chose me in Christ to be holy in your presence, you nourish me with your Body and Blood so that I will have life in me, and you send me to be your witness before men and to bear fruit that will last.

I ask you with utter trust and confidence for the grace I need to be generous, to say yes to all you have been insisting on during this retreat, and definitively to incorporate it into my life.

I want to love you more like you deserve to be loved, not as someone I find useful, but as the one who loved me like no one else ever has or can. The more I look at you, the more I realized my nothingness, my smallness, my need for your grace.

I thank you; how can I ever stop thanking you and praising you for all you have done for me?

Mary, faithful mother, God entrusted his Son to you. I place myself too in your hands. Help me to listen to his Spirit as faithfully as you did as I make my resolutions at the end of this retreat.

SCRIPTURE PASSAGE

"There was a large crowd gathering and people from every town finding their way to him, he told this parable. A sower went out to sow a seed. Now, as he sowed, some fell on the edge of the path and were trampled on and the birds of the air ate it up. Some seed fell on rock and when it came up it withered away having no moisture. Some seed fell in the middle of thorns and the thorns grew with it and choked it. And some seed fell into good soil and grew and produced its crop a hundred fold. And saying this he cried, 'Anyone who has ears for listening should listen.'"

Now, his disciples were a little mystified with this and couldn't see what he was getting at, so they asked him, and Jesus goes on to explain:

"'This then is what the parable means. The seed is the word of God, those on the edge of the path are people who hear it and then the devil comes and carries away the word from their hearts, in case they should believe and be saved. Those on the rock are people who when they first hear it welcome the word with joy but they have no root. They believe for a while and in times of trial they give up. As for the part that fell into thorns, this is people who have heard but as they go on their way they are choked by the worries and riches and the pleasures of life, and they never produce crops. As for the part in rich soil, this is the people with a noble and generous heart who have heard the word and take it to themselves and yield a harvest through their perseverance.'"

EXPLORE THE MEANING
AND MESSAGES OF THE PASSAGE

Jesus tells us that the seed is the word of God. We have spent our retreat listening to the Word of God. God has spent these days sowing his word in our heart. So he's talking about us as he describes the four types of men, the four types of hearer. The first three are lessons in the dangers we face, ways in which the retreat will bear no fruit, and the fourth is what we should strive to be; it is Jesus' recipe for success.

1. The naïve

"A sower went out to sow a seed, as he sowed some fell on the edge of the path and were trampled on, and the birds of the air ate it up... Those on the edge of the path are people that have heard it, but then the devil comes and carries away the word from their hearts in case they should believe and be saved."

The first person Jesus considers and tells us not to become is the naïve man who forgets that his Christian life, his vocation, and the new leaf he wants to turn over in his life are all in constant danger. He forgets we have an active enemy who tempts us over and over again, is cunning, sowing bad seed alongside the good to choke it out, and trying to steal the seed before it even has time to set down roots.

We often think that our spiritual work and our following of Christ is something "between me and God alone." God sends his grace and we correspond, and if there is a problem, it must be either me or God. And so when we find the going difficult, we tend to think, "Maybe God doesn't want this of me any more." That applies to our reactions to difficulties in marriage, the priesthood, and consecrated life, and our difficulties in carrying out our resolutions. We totally forget about the third person, not the Holy Spirit, but the enemy of our soul.

They say the greatest triumph of the devil is when he gets us to think and act as if he didn't exist. Jesus warns us against this.

We have to protect his word in our lives. The enemy is active. He is there and his purpose is to take the seed out of our souls, lest we believe, put it into action, and be saved. He is not there by accident but with a purpose, to steal the Word from out of our hearts. I decide my call is to consecrate my life to God, but then a wonderful person of the opposite sex comes into my life, and immediately I think it is a sign from God. This happens when we forget that our vocation has an enemy.

Jesus is warning us so this won't happen to us. On our own, we forget that the enemy doesn't want us to follow what Christ wants us to do. He tries everything to take away God's seed and then sows his own doubts in our mind. Really, we can't make much sense of what happens to us in our life if we don't remember that the devil exists, and that his purpose is to thwart our belief and stop his word from bearing fruit in our life.

Sometimes he is very direct in his attacks; at others very subtle, attacking under the guise of good. He gets us to watch out for ourselves, to take care of ourselves. He sows temptation and doubt, making us think we are not worthy of what God wants us to do and getting us to turn away. So when we feel like changing direction, we have to ask ourselves always, "Could that not be the Enemy's voice, luring me away, taking God's seed from my heart?" We already know that we're not worthy. Could the one who is making us waver be the enemy of our souls, since our weakness is no news to God who called us?

2. The man driven by his feelings

"Some of the seed fell on rocky ground, and when it came up, it withered away because it had no moisture…. Those on the rock are people who, when they first hear it welcome the word with joy, but they have no root. They believe for a while and then, in times of trial, they give up."

Here is the second type of person Jesus doesn't want us to become, and to our dismay it refers to something that many would equate with being fervent, religious, and sensitive. We are talking about the person who seems to spring into life, bubbling over with enthusiasm, at the drop of a hat.

It is all too common to make religion consist in some externals and our feelings. We "had a good Mass" or a "good retreat" if the whole experience moved us and made us feel good and fervent. We expect always to be moved in the same way, and if we don't feel the same force of emotions, it feels like God is no longer with us.

By no means is Jesus saying that emotions are wrong. The fact is that when we first realize the truth of his love and our redemption, it fills us with joy to the point that we can seriously doubt that it is his message if it does not bring us joy.

Jesus does warn us against being of stone, where his Word cannot take root, of making it all consist in emotions and feelings to the point that his cross cannot be planted, and there is a little bit of this in all of us. This is a problem, because in addition to the great joy of Bethlehem, his path and the path of his disciples also winds through the Garden of Gethsemane to Calvary before reaching the joy without end of the Resurrection.

The comparison Jesus makes is jolting. He tells us that the person for whom all has to be good feelings is like a stone. So the man who thinks every confession and Communion are going to be like the first day of his entrance into the Church, or the priest who thinks every day has to feel like his ordination day, or the newlywed that expects every day to be full of confetti, sun, music, and champagne is in Jesus' estimation like a stone. But a stone is unfeeling! Precisely.

The man who bases everything on his own feelings is the most hardened egotist, with no room for others in his heart, no feelings or room for others, much less for the Cross.

If it makes him feel good, he'll do it; if God gives plenty of satisfaction, he will follow—as long as there is no darkness, no cross; as long as all is joy, miracles, and success. Nothing can penetrate such selfishness. Even the initial good fruits must shrivel and die. All it takes is a little difficulty, a little testing, "a time of trial"....

Can you bring yourself to kneel down beside Christ in Gethsemane and say, "Lord, I want to suffer your passion with you, I want to stand by you even if it means being ridiculed and left by my friends, even if it means persecution and giving up things I'm so attached to. But by giving them up, I can give myself more to you"?

This is why God allows trials. It the only way for us to leave ourselves and possess him. It is the only way to true happiness. When we have difficulties, we should thank God. What does somebody who is training do the first time he gets out and tries to run around the track? One lap, and he is dead for the rest of the day. If he wants to run a mile he will do it again, and then again. Hard things get easy only when we tackle them, not when we run from them. Trials are God's way of taking the center off ourselves and turning the rock that is in our soul into better ground.

3. Too busy

"As for the part that fell into thorns, this is people who have heard. But as they go on their way they are choked by the worries, and riches, and pleasures of this life, and never produce any crop."

Here is the third mistake we can make. The ground the seed fell upon is basically good ground where the seed could take root, like the many other plants growing there. The enemy can't get at it, and the ground is not rocky. So, what is wrong?

This person does not reject the word, but there are just so many other things going on in his life that the word cannot bear fruit.

So many other things—not necessarily bad things, for what life is there without worries? And we need possessions to live... and pleasure in itself is not bad, for all good things give a pleasure of their own.

The problem is that there is no room for the Word. You're not saying no to God, but you have so many things to take care of that you cannot fit in your yes.

That's when good things become bad for us, when they don't leave room for better and more important things.

Here is an important question to ask yourself and to find an answer to before you leave here today. God has spoken to you. There is something you want to do or change or follow through on, something he is asking of you. It is the seed, God's word to you, and you are willing to do it; you are not going to let the enemy come and take it out of your heart. Now, the question is, are you going to let the seed grow? Will you make room for it in your life? Will you make room for prayer, for the sacraments, for time each day to spend with our Lord?

Of course you want to, so ask yourself what things are most likely to crop up to cause you to never quite get around to it?

If you don't make time for prayer, the Mass, the Rosary, for time with Jesus, he is warning you that the seed will not be able to bear fruit. It will be choked by all the other things you have to do.

4. The true disciple

"As for the part in rich soil, this is the people with a noble and generous heart who have heard the word and take it to themselves and yield a harvest through their perseverance."

They bear fruit not because they are blessed and lucky, and things are much easier for them than they are for us, but through their perseverance.

After describing the struggles that we go through (our struggle with Christ's enemy, with our emotions, and with those things that crush in and don't let the seed grow), Jesus goes on to paint for us the picture of the disciple he wants each one of us to be.

Let's look at the description of this person. It is no bed of roses. It involves work, but it yields the fruit we are all seeking.

We have to start off by cultivating "a noble heart." That is, to have an honest heart, a true conscience with a sense for what is right and what is wrong, a heart that loves what is beautiful, just, and virtuous. I think all of us would love others to find precisely that when they look inside our spirit.

And Jesus adds, "a generous heart." Like his, a heart that is willing to give of itself, that is outward-looking and not self-centered. A person others feel blessed to know.

Jesus envisions us doing two very distinct things. First, to "listen to the word." So often we think God is not talking because we can't hear him, but the reason really is that we are not listening. Hasn't he told us to love one another as he has loved us, and to pray for those who do us wrong? Now, have we listened? The apostles heard Christ speaking about his Passion and death over and over, yet they never really listened to him, and their world fell apart when it happened. Some people get discouraged when the Church is attacked and persecuted, yet Christ said, "If they have persecuted me they will persecute you." We need to listen.

Second, to "take it [the word] to ourselves." This means to say, "Yes, he is speaking to me," and apply it to ourselves. It means to take what he says, and go and do it. "Go you and do the same."

Then, finally, the great challenge: after listening and realizing he is speaking to us, and after our first burst of fervor to do what he wants, he expects us to "yield a harvest through perseverance."

Here is the key. It is easy to say "I love you" on a wedding day, but it is something else to repeat it when "for richer or poorer, in sickness and in health" become realities. It is easy to say to our Lord on professions day, "I am all yours," and something else to rise each day for him, to weather temptation and opposition, to serve him in others day in and day out, year in and year out.

The problem is not that we don't start out on the journey; the problem is we give up. Perseverance is the great challenge, and final perseverance is a grace.

CONCLUSIONS

Go over in your mind with Christ which of the pictures he paints and the warnings he gives applies to you, probably a mix. Speak to him about it. Ask him pardon, and make your resolution. Decide the time you are going to dedicate to him each day, and make a firm resolution to persevere in your efforts.

Take time as well to glance back over the retreat and see what he has most insisted upon, the recurrent thoughts that have entered your soul as you went from one meditation to the next, and the inspirations and good resolutions he placed in your heart.

If you have any questions about anything, speak to your spiritual director.

And take a look towards tomorrow.

FINAL CONVERSATION WITH CHRIST

You promise abundant fruit to those who persevere. I am so weak and inconsistent, but I really want to live my one and only life for you. I am not looking for the glamour of following you, I simply want to be with you always and to do your will.

I want you to be able to depend on me, and I will always depend on you.

RESOLUTIONS

Lastly, write down a select few final resolutions and put them where you will see them every day as a reminder of what you want to do for Christ.

Include something you are going to do in your prayer life and your relationship with Christ, something you will do in your dealings with others, and something you will do to be a more active apostle.

And set out with trust and hope.